P9-DYZ-245

The best
family
slow cooker
recipes

The best
family
slow cooker
recipes

Donna-Marie Pye

Robert
ROSE

The Best Family Slow Cooker Recipes
Text copyright © 2003 Donna-Marie Pye
Photographs copyright © 2003 Robert Rose Inc.

No part of this publication may be reproduced, stored in a retrieval system or transmitted, in any form or by any means, without the prior written consent of the publisher or a licence from The Canadian Copyright Licensing Agency (Access Copyright). For an Access Copyright licence, visit www.accesscopyright.ca or call toll free to 1-800-893-5777.

For complete cataloguing information, see page 185.

Disclaimer
The recipes in this book have been carefully tested by our kitchen and our tasters. To the best of our knowledge, they are safe and nutritious for ordinary use and users. For those people with food or other allergies, or who have special food requirements or health issues, please read the suggested contents of each recipe carefully and determine whether or not they may create a problem for you. All recipes are used at the risk of the consumer. Consumers should consult their slow cooker manufacturer's manual for recommended procedures and cooking times.

We cannot be responsible for any hazards, loss or damage that may occur as a result of any recipe use.

For those with special needs, allergies, requirements or health problems, in the event of any doubt, please contact your medical advisor prior to the use of any recipe.

Design & Production: PageWave Graphics Inc.
Editorial: Shelley Tanaka
Recipe Testing: Jennifer MacKenzie
Photography: Mark T. Shapiro
Food Styling: Kate Bush
Prop Styling: Charlene Erricson
Color Scans: Colour Technologies

Cover image: Chicken Cacciatore (page 58)

The publisher and author wish to express their appreciation to the following suppliers of props used in the food photography:

DISHES, LINENS AND ACCESSORIES

Caban
396 St. Clair Avenue West
Toronto, Ontario M5P 3N3
Tel: 416-654-3316
www.clubmonaco.com

Homefront
371 Eglinton Avenue West
Toronto, Ontario M5N 1A3
Tel: 416-488-3189
www.homefrontshop.com

FLATWARE

Gourmet Settings Inc.
245 West Beaver Creek Road, Unit 10
Richmond Hill, Ontario L4B 1L1
Tel: 1-800-551-2649
www.gourmetsettings.com

We acknowledge the financial support of the Government of Canada through the Book Publishing Industry Development Program (BPIDP) for our publishing activities.

Published by Robert Rose Inc.
120 Eglinton Avenue East, Suite 800, Toronto, Ontario, Canada M4P 1E2
Tel: (416) 322-6552; Fax: (416) 322-6936

Printed in Canada
1 2 3 4 5 6 7 8 9 10 GP 11 10 09 08 07 06 05 04 03

To Lawrence, Darcy and Jack — my most inspiring and discerning audience. You make it all worthwhile!

I also dedicate this book to the memory of Victoria D'Agostino, whose creative food combinations always brought a smile to my face.

Contents

Acknowledgments

One might think delivering a sequel to be much easier than writing a first book. However, just as having a second baby can throw you for a loop, writing a sequel posed its own special challenges. The biggest was my desire to maintain a high level of creativity — to deliver a fresh and exciting collection of recipes for a tried-and-true kitchen appliance. To do this, I relied on the input of many people, especially the readers of my first book, *Best Slow Cooker Recipes*. I very much appreciate all your thoughts and comments, and especially your questions, as they gave me a clear picture of what you were looking for in a slow cooker cookbook.

Once again, thanks go to the entire Robert Rose creative team, especially Bob Dees and Marian Jarkovich, who have produced another great-looking, exceptionally edited cookbook; Jennifer MacKenzie for her impeccable recipe standards and fine-tuned palate, and for ensuring that everything was tested-till-perfect; Shelley Tanaka for her superb editing and being a pleasure to work with; the design team at PageWave Graphics — Andrew Smith, Joseph Gisini, Kevin Cockburn and Daniella Zanchetta — for turning type into beautiful design; Kate Bush, Mark Shapiro and Charlene Erricson, the picture experts who worked their magic and made everything look so good.

I am also blessed to be surrounded by such a supportive group of friends; without their assistance this project would not have been possible. My thanks go to my good friend Carol Parsons, who spent much of her time over the summer in the sweltering heat happily testing and tasting recipes for me. Your assistance was invaluable, as were your ever-shining smile and positive encouragement. Thanks to Joanne Burton, who took on the task of typing the first draft at the same time that she was launching a scrapbooking business, and to Dale Burgoyne, who typed the second draft while taking care of a new baby. I couldn't have done it without you. Thanks to my fellow home economist and colleague Barb Holland for her proofreading help. And finally, special thanks go to Karen Scian for her unwavering support and assistance. If it didn't taste good, smell good and look and sound just right, she would always let me know!

Thanks also to the countless family members, neighbors and friends for their encouragement, suggestions and offers to sample many of the recipes, and to those who presented me with ideas and recipes for this book. I have tried to incorporate as many as possible and give credit where credit is due.

In the end I have to thank my family, who supported me while my life revolved around this book. They have been the best family any wife and mom could have — quietly patient while I have been writing, and uncomplaining when I placed yet another slow cooker meal in front of them. Cheer up, Darcy and Jack. We will all eat a good steak dinner soon! And to my husband, Lawrence Greaves (most people think he eats like a king every night, but if they only knew) — after fifteen years, you have more patience than I deserve.

✑ Introduction

Since writing *Best Slow Cooker Recipes*, I have become even more convinced of the wonderful benefits of the slow cooker. My love affair with the appliance began many years ago when I commuted to a job that was a lengthy drive from my home. To have a tasty home-cooked meal on the dinner table, I would use my slow cooker at least once a week.

Today, though I no longer commute, I am a freelance home economist, busy wife and mother to two children aged ten and seven. With their array of after-school activities, I continue to use my slow cooker, looking for new and creative ways to feed my on-the-go family.

While most of us like to eat, we are all challenged by the stress of thinking about what to make for dinner every night. That's why more and more people are once again discovering the benefits of slow cookers. Introduced more than thirty years ago as a device for cooking beans, today's slow cooker has undergone various improvements and innovations. However, it continues to be an effective time-management tool no kitchen should be without. After all, who doesn't want to come home to a hot home-cooked meal at the end of the day?

This collection of recipes includes traditional family favorites as well as dishes that reflect our ever-expanding multicultural world. I still love a simple meatloaf (page 84) or macaroni and cheese (page 138). However, I can also travel to all corners of the globe — to the Orient for shredded pork flavored with hoisin and ginger (page 112), to India for a savory mulligatawny soup (page 40), or to Russia for borscht (page 49). I have included some of my favorite desserts here, too, such as an unbelievable slow cooker cheesecake (page 172), and a few condiments and snacks that store well.

Slow cooker dishes have always been ideal for social gatherings, and a great way to share food with friends. They are perfect for toting to potlucks, work functions and church events. With more than 6 million slow cookers being sold in North America every year, consumers are finding more ways to use this handy household appliance. For this reason, I have included a chapter called Entertaining with Your Slow Cooker, designed especially for those occasions when you are faced with the question, "What should I take to…?"

I hope you enjoy this new collection of slow cooker recipes and will come to rely on your slow cooker for creating stress-free home-cooked meals.

Donna-Marie Pye

Using Your Slow Cooker

Slow cooking is for everyone — families, couples, singles, students and seniors. Whether you are on a tight schedule or love leisurely cooking, slow cookers can provide good, healthy food without requiring you to spend hours over a hot stove.

The basic premise is simple. Assemble and prepare the ingredients at your convenience — whether it's the night before or earlier in the day — place them in the slow cooker stoneware, turn it on and let the food cook while you walk away. Delicious aromas greet you when you return at the end of the day. Toss a salad and pour the drinks, and a delicious, home-prepared meal is ready for you to serve and savor.

Benefits of Slow Cooking

After many years of slow cooking, and two cookbooks later, I am even more convinced of the marvelous benefits of this appliance. Not only are slow cookers convenient and portable, but cooking foods at low heat produces flavorful, tender results. Slow cooking tenderizes tougher cuts of meat by cooking them in their own juices and slowly breaking down the tough connective tissues. Stews and chilis don't dry out or stick to the bottom of the pot, and the even, low temperature ensures perfect results with more delicate dishes such as puddings and custards.

How Does It Work?

The slow cooker is a simple appliance that is relatively low tech. The appliance consists of a metal casing, stoneware insert and tight-fitting glass or plastic lid. The low-wattage metal casing houses electric heating elements between the inner and outer sides. As the elements heat up, they warm the insulated air trapped between the metal walls, ultimately heating the metal. Heat is then transferred to the cushion of air between the inner metal wall and the stoneware. Because the heating elements never make direct contact with the stoneware, there are no hot spots, eliminating the need for constant stirring. Slow cookers use about the same amount of energy as a 100-watt lightbulb — substantially less than a conventional oven.

Types of Slow Cookers

The first slow cooker was introduced in 1971 as the Rival Company's Crock-Pot ®. While the original slow cooker came in only one size, today's models come in a variety of sizes, from tiny 1-quart to large 7-quart capacity. The smaller sizes are ideal for sauces and dips, while the larger ones are good for whole roasts and desserts. For convenience and ease of cleaning, look for a model with the removable stoneware insert.

Many people own more than one slow cooker. Our two-person household outgrew our original $3\frac{1}{2}$-quart size as our family grew. I now rely on larger slow cookers to feed my active growing family. Most of the recipes in this book have been developed using a 4- and 6-quart size — the most popular models on the market today — but many can be made in a range of sizes. Check the guidelines at the beginning of each recipe for the suggested slow cooker size. The size and shape of the dish are likely to affect the cooking times; in general, the smaller the slow cooker, the shorter the cooking time.

Some manufacturers sell a multipurpose cooker, which can fulfill a variety of functions such as browning, sautéing, boiling, braising, simmering and deep-frying. While these can be used for certain types of slow cooking, they are not suited to all slow cooker recipes. In these models, the heating element is located in the base of the housing unit, so the appliance cooks with direct heat. Unlike slow cookers, the multipurpose cookers require supervision and stirring, since foods tend to stick to the bottom. When used for slow cooking, these cookers are best suited to soups and stews. Because of the direct heat, liquids tend to evaporate quickly, and foods can't always endure the long hours slow cooking requires.

Your manufacturer's instruction booklet will give you further information on how best to care for and clean your slow cooker. It is important to read these instructions carefully before embarking on your first recipe. Other variables that can affect the cooking time are extreme humidity, power fluctuations and high altitudes. Caution should be taken if these factors affect you.

TIPS FOR SUCCESSFUL SLOW COOKING

The slow cooker can save you precious time while creating delicious and nutritious dishes. However, there are tips that will help you use the appliance to its best advantage.

Brown Meats and Poultry and Sauté Vegetables First

In general, it is a good idea to brown meats before adding them to the slow cooker. Although this step may add a few extra minutes in preparation time, browning dramatically improves the end result. Not only does it improve the color by caramelizing the meat, it also breaks down the natural sugars and releases their flavors. Sautéing vegetables with spices and dried herbs before slow cooking also produces a richer, more intense sauce.

To brown meats and sauté vegetables add a small amount of oil to a large nonstick skillet or Dutch oven. Heat over medium-high heat, then add the food. Brown meat in small batches, otherwise the meat will steam rather than brown. Stir or turn frequently to brown evenly on all sides, then transfer to the slow cooker. Dredge meat in seasoned flour before cooking rather than after to reduce the chance of lumpy gravy.

To maximize flavor, deglaze the pan with either wine or broth after browning. Simply pour a small amount of liquid into the skillet, stirring to remove the caramelized juices and cooked-on food particles. Bring to a boil, reduce heat and simmer for one to two minutes while stirring. Pour this liquid over the meat in the slow cooker.

Don't Overdo the Liquid

One of the first things you will notice about slow cooking is the amount of liquid that accumulates inside the pot. Because the slow cooker cooks at low heat, liquid doesn't evaporate as it does in dry heat cooking. Since the steam cannot escape as it rises, it collects under the lid, dripping back down into the cooking liquid. This can make the cooking juices more watery. For this reason, most slow cooker recipes, with the exception of soups, stews and sauces, call for about half as much liquid as conventional recipes.

If there is too much liquid at the end of the cooking time, remove the lid, increase the temperature to **High** and cook uncovered for 30 to 45 minutes to reduce the liquid. Alternatively, remove the solid contents with a slotted spoon and cover to keep warm. Pour the cooking liquid into a saucepan and reduce on the stovetop over high heat until the sauce cooks down to the desired consistency.

Always Cook Covered

Always cook with the slow cooker lid on. Most slow cookers have a heavy glass or plastic lid to trap the heat as it rises and convert it into steam. This is in fact what cooks the food. Removing the lid will result in major heat losses (which the slow cooker can't quickly recover), ultimately affecting the cooking time. Lift the lid only when it is time to check for doneness, when adding ingredients or when stirring is recommended.

Cut Vegetables into Same-sized Pieces

Raw vegetables often take longer to cook in a slow cooker than meat and poultry. Root vegetables such as carrots, parsnips, turnips and potatoes simmer rather than boil in the cooking liquid. For this reason, food should be cut into uniform pieces no larger than 1-inch (2.5-cm) cubes. It is best to place them as close as possible to the bottom and sides of the stoneware bowl, so that they benefit from close contact to the heat source.

Observe Recommended Cooking Temperatures and Times

The slow cooker works by simmering food at a constant low temperature. The **Low** setting cooks food at about 200°F (100°C), and the **High** setting cooks food at about 300°F (150°C). However, the cooking temperatures of different makes and models can vary. When you first start to use your slow cooker, check foods after the minimum recommended cooking time. You will soon find out how fast your slow cooker cooks, and you can adjust the cooking times if necessary.

In recipes where only one temperature is given, cook on that temperature. This is especially important for appetizers and desserts, where overcooking or undercooking can affect the quality of the finished dish. For the most tender results, tougher cuts of meat such as pot roasts and stewing meat are often best cooked on the **Low** setting.

Many people want to turn on their slow cooker in the morning before going to work and come home nine or ten hours later to a hot, ready-to-eat meal. Many of the main-course dishes and main-course soups in this book can be cooked this long at **Low**, though they may also be ready to eat several hours earlier (in these cases a wide range of cooking times may be indicated). However, some foods, such as chicken and pork chops, do not stand up to longer cooking times. Bean dishes may also become very soft if cooked for a long time. You will soon find out how to best use the slow cooker to cook foods to your own taste.

Season Liberally

Because slow cooker foods cook longer than they do using conventional methods, it is best to use dried herb leaves and whole or crushed spices rather than ground herbs and spices. In general, fresh herbs such as basil and cilantro should be added during the last hour of cooking. Always taste the finished dish before serving and adjust the seasoning as needed.

Using Additional Dishes and Pans

In conventional cooking, foods like custards, puddings and cheesecakes are often baked in a hot water bath or bain-marie. This involves placing the filled baking dish in another pan filled with hot water. Heat is transferred from the hot water to the custard, cooking it gently and slowly so that it doesn't curdle or form a crust.

The water bath technique works beautifully in the slow cooker. Custards, puddings and cheesecakes stay creamy and smooth, and cheesecakes do not crack.

The challenge is finding a dish that will fit properly in the slow cooker. First, you will need a large round or oval slow cooker. Smaller cookers will usually only accommodate a dish or pan purchased from the slow cooker manufacturer or an old-fashioned pudding mold with a lid. Standard 4-cup (1 L) or 6-cup (1.5 L) ovenproof baking bowls work well in most larger slow cookers. If you are making a cheesecake, a 7- or 8-inch (17 or 20 cm) springform pan should fit in nicely.

To remove a pan from the slow cooker easily, make foil handles. Cut a 2-foot (60 cm) piece of foil in half lengthwise. Fold each strip in half lengthwise and crisscross the strips under the pan. Bring the strips up the sides of the pan and tuck the ends inside the lid. Use the foil handles as lifters to remove the pan from the slow cooker. You can also line the slow cooker with a double thickness of cheesecloth to help you lift. Both of these methods will save you from having to awkwardly remove the dish using spatulas or oven mitts.

Make Ahead

The biggest challenge to slow cooking is being organized enough to have everything ready in advance. If you need to start your slow cooker early in the day, try preparing a few things the night before:

- Pre-chop carrots, celery and other ingredients and refrigerate until the next day.
- Defrost frozen vegetables overnight in the refrigerator.
- Trim and cut (but do not brown) meat and poultry.
- Assemble non-perishable ingredients and cooking utensils in a convenient spot for a quick start.

In this book, recipes that especially lend themselves to some advance preparation or cooking are accompanied by **Make Ahead** instructions. Many recipes can also be completely cooked in advance and stored in the refrigerator or freezer for future use.

FOOD SAFETY

According to the U.S. Department of Agriculture, bacteria is killed at a temperature of 165°F (74°C). In a slow cooker that is used properly (i.e., the lid is left on and food is cooked at the appropriate heat level for the appropriate length of time), foods will reach their safe internal cooked temperature quickly enough to inhibit bacterial growth. To make sure the slow cooker can effectively transfer heat from the metal walls to the stoneware insert and then to the food, do not fill the cooker more than three-quarters full, and always cook with the lid on.

Safety Tips

- Always start with fresh or defrosted meat and poultry. Using frozen or partially frozen meat will increase the time required for the temperature to reach the "safe zone" where bacteria growth is inhibited.
- In general, defrost frozen vegetables like peas and beans before adding them to the slow cooker, to prevent them from slowing the cooking process. Defrost in the refrigerator overnight or place under cold running water to thaw and separate.
- Cook all ground meat or poultry completely before adding it to the slow cooker. (The exception to this is meatloaf, and proper cooking directions are given for this in the individual recipes.) If you are cooking the ground meat the night before, chill it separately before combining it with other ingredients in the slow cooker.
- Do not refrigerate uncooked or partially cooked meat or poultry in the slow cooker stoneware, as the insert will become very cold and will slow the cooking process. Partially cook meat or poultry only when adding immediately to the slow cooker. Do not refrigerate for later cooking.
- Meats and vegetables that have been pre-cut should be stored separately in the refrigerator. After cutting uncooked meat, never use the same cutting board or knife for other foods without thoroughly washing them with soap and hot water between uses.
- When cooking whole poultry and meatloaf, use a meat thermometer to accurately test doneness. Insert the thermometer into the thickest part of the thigh or loaf to ensure that the temperature has reached 170°F (77°C).
- Do not lift the lid of the slow cooker while the food is cooking. Every time you remove the lid, the slow cooker takes about 20 minutes to recover its cooking temperature.
- Remove leftovers from the stoneware and refrigerate as quickly as possible.
- Do not reheat cooked food in the slow cooker. Leftovers can be defrosted in the refrigerator or microwave and then reheated in a conventional or microwave oven or in a saucepan on the stove.

Entertaining with Your Slow Cooker

You're heading off to a special get-together and you've volunteered to bring something yummy for the buffet table. But it has been a busy week, and you haven't had time to really think about it. What are you going to do?

Enter your lifesaver, the slow cooker. While most of us have a hard time trying to figure out what we're going to have for dinner every night, choosing the perfect dish to offer to friends and company can be even harder.

Potlucks provide the perfect opportunity to use your slow cooker. It is a great time saver and it will free up important oven space that is needed for other dishes. And, of course, you can serve directly from your slow cooker, which saves on extra dishes and eases clean-up. I often use my slow cooker for entertaining, both at home and at outside events.

Tips for Transporting Your Slow Cooker

- Wrap the slow cooker in a towel or in newspapers for insulation, then place in a box (or other container) that will stay flat in your car. Some slow cooker manufacturers sell insulated totes that perfectly hold a slow cooker. You may want to consider investing in one if you travel with yours a lot.
- Attach rubber bands around the handles and lid to secure the lid.
- Serve the food within an hour or plug in the slow cooker and set on **Low** or **Keep Warm** so it will stay warm.

What should I take to...?

Here are a few popular situations where your slow cooker could come in handy, along with suggestions for recipes suited to the occasion, whether you are the host or you have to tote along.

Superbowl Party

What would a football party be without a big pot of simmering chili? Prepare it early in the day so it is ready for the halftime show. Be sure to include some crusty rolls, or make a batch of cornbread a day ahead. Include some dips and appetizers for snacking on during the game (some of which can be made up to a week in advance). And, of course, don't forget to provide a good selection of beer!

- Hot Corn Dip (page 23)
- Nacho Cheese Dip (page 24)
- Bourbon Bangers (page 25)

- Best Beer Nuts (page 30)
- Easy-on-Ya Lasagna (page 99)
- Rock'n and Roast'n Chili (page 106)
- Tailgating Four-Bean Hot Dish (page 144)
- Vegetable Chili with Sour Cream Topping (page 148)
- Johnnycake Cornbread (page 153)

Winter Warm-up

Nothing warms those cold feet and hands after a day of winter activities like a piping hot bowl of soup or a thick, hearty stew. Prepare it in the morning and let it cook while you are out having fun. When you return, serve it with a green salad and a crusty loaf of bread for an easy one-pot meal. Add some excitement for the kids with a delicious and fun fondue. Or walk in the door to a welcoming hot drink or warm dessert.

- Mulled Raspberry Tea (page 32)
- Cabbage Roll Soup (page 34)
- Mahogany Beef Stew (page 92)
- Cider Pork Stew (page 110)
- Pizza Fondue (page 135)
- Apricot Croissant Pudding with Caramel Sauce (page 170)
- Double Berry Maple Crumble (page 174)

Aces Are Wild

Everyone is a winner when friends and family come together for games and good food, whether you're playing billiards, cards, board games or hamming it up with a karaoke machine. Keep the food simple with a buffet of tasty appetizers that you can eat with toothpicks and napkins.

- Roadhouse-style Spinach and Artichoke Dip (page 22)
- Nacho Cheese Dip (page 24)
- Bourbon Bangers (page 25)
- Fruity Glazed Meatballs (page 26)
- Turkish Winglets (page 27)
- Best Beer Nuts (page 30)
- Pizza Fondue (page 135)

Summer Celebrations

Summer is always a popular time to reconnect with young and old, whether it's a family reunion, Father's Day celebration or visiting a friend's summer cottage. While barbecuing is popular, some days can be too hot for you to stand over a sweltering grill, so slow cookers can be the answer. Ingredients are farm fresh and perfect for delicious slow-cooked one-dish meals and desserts. Be sure to serve lots of coleslaw (page 57) and jugs of lemonade.

- Slow Cooker-to-Grill Sticky Ribs (page 117)
- Pulled Pork Fajitas (page 124)
- Slow-cooked Macaroni and Cheese (page 138)
- Cowpoke Baked Beans (page 140)
- Plum Cobbler (page 179)
- Pineapple Upside-down Cake (page 182)

Book Club Night

Make use of your slow cooker at your monthly book club meetings. That way you can spend more time enjoying the discussion instead of being in the kitchen preparing the meal.

- Roadhouse-style Spinach and Artichoke Dip (page 22)
- Sun-dried Tomato Appetizer Cheesecake (page 28)
- Chocolate Chai Tea (page 31)
- Mulled Raspberry Tea (page 32)
- Chicken with Orange Gremolata (page 66)
- Vegetable-stuffed Chicken with Mushroom Sauce (page 71)
- Spinach and Prosciutto Turkey Rolls (page 76)
- Perfectly Poached Salmon (page 146)
- Honey Lemon Beets (page 156)
- Barley Mushroom "Risotto" (page 162)
- Middle Eastern Pilaf (page 163)
- Wild Rice Stuffing with Almonds and Cranberries (page 165)
- Bananas with Honey-roasted Nuts (page 169)
- Basic-but-Beautiful Slow Cooker Cheesecake (page 172)

Especially for Kids

Whether you are throwing a back-to-school brunch for your children and their friends, looking for perfect party food for a group of teens or serving a Friday night meal to the family, here are some kid-friendly recipes everyone will enjoy, from make-ahead foods that can be packed into lunch boxes to keep-warm main dishes for families on the fly.

- Hot Corn Dip (page 23)
- Nacho Cheese Dip (page 24)
- Easy Wieners and Beaners Soup (page 37)

- Clubhouse Chicken (page 59)
- PBJ Chicken Stew (page 64)
- Anthony's Big Ragu (page 82)
- Beef and Bean Burritos (page 83)
- Easy-on-Ya Lasagna (page 99)
- Tortilla Stack (page 100)
- Double Decker Spicy Pork Tacos (page 111)
- Ginger Pork Wraps (page 112)
- Slow Cooker-to-Grill Sticky Ribs (page 117)
- Pulled Pork Fajitas (page 124)
- Banana Walnut French Toast (page 134)
- Pizza Fondue (page 135)
- Slow-cooked Macaroni and Cheese (page 138)
- Good Morning Granola (page 150)
- Maple Pecan Multigrain Porridge (page 151)
- Johnnycake Cornbread (page 153)
- Veggie-stuffed Baked Potatoes (page 160)

The Perfect Potluck

Community potlucks and church suppers give everyone a chance to show off their talents, and many recipes have been exchanged and passed down through generations as a result of such occasions. The most popular, of course, is the classic casserole, and the slow cooker makes toting these a breeze.

- Bourbon Bangers (page 25)
- Fruity Glazed Meatballs (page 26)
- Turkish Winglets (page 27)
- Polenta Tamale Pie (page 65)
- Cheesy Pesto Pasta (page 69)
- Creamy White Chicken Chili (page 72)
- Turkey Tetrazzini (page 79)
- Sauerbraten Beef Stew (page 95)
- Nancy's Rouladen (page 96)
- Easy-on-Ya Lasagna (page 99)
- Adobe Pork and Bean Chili (page 127)
- Pizza Fondue (page 135)
- Corn and Green Chili Tamale Casserole (page 136)
- Creamy Spinach Ricotta Noodles (page 137)
- Cowpoke Baked Beans (page 140)
- Apricot Croissant Pudding with Caramel Sauce (page 170)
- Plum Cobbler (page 179)
- Old-fashioned Gingerbread with Lemon Sauce (page 180)

Holiday Specials

Holiday celebrations mean lots of friends, family, fun and food. Of course, the turkey and stuffing are a given, but oven space is always at a premium. Take advantage of your slow cooker to prepare a few appetizers or condiments a day or two ahead, make the stuffing in the morning and have it warming during the day or keep a hot drink simmering. Have a Tourtière Shepherd's Pie (page 126) waiting at home after church on Christmas Eve. Or use your slow cooker to serve up a soup for starters, to prepare an extra dessert or separate entree for vegetarians, or to use as an extra server for a delicious array of side dishes.

Appetizers and Condiments
- Sun-dried Tomato Appetizer Cheesecake (page 28)
- Olives in Red Wine (page 29)
- Mulled Raspberry Tea (page 32)
- Rhubarb Apple Sauce (page 166)

Soups
- Roasted Pear and Parsnip Soup (page 46)
- Southwestern Pumpkin Soup (page 47)
- Spicy Sweet Potato Soup (page 48)

Stuffings and Side Dishes
- Braised Cabbage and Raspberries (page 154)
- Scalloped Corn (page 155)
- Scalloped Sweet Potatoes and Parsnips (page 157)
- Oktoberfest Hot Potato Salad (page 159)
- Lisa's Classic Green Beans (page 161)
- Country-style Sage and Bread Stuffing (page 164)
- Wild Rice Stuffing with Almonds and Cranberries (page 165)

Desserts
- Amaretti Pear Crisp (page 168)
- Basic-but-Beautiful Slow Cooker Cheesecake (page 172)
- Double Chocolate Caramel Bread Pudding (page 176)
- Maple-sauced Pears (page 177)
- Pumpkin Pie Custard Dessert (page 184)

Great Beginnings

Roadhouse-style Spinach and Artichoke Dip

Makes about 3 cups (750 mL)

This is one of my favorite appetizers when we have games nights with friends. It tastes just like the dip served in roadhouse-style restaurants. Serve with warm pita triangles, tortilla chips, breadsticks, pretzels or slices of crusty baguette.

Different brands of artichoke hearts have different flavors, which will affect the taste of this dip (some taste more vinegary than others). Use your favorite brand; you could also use marinated artichokes.

Roasted Red Pepper and Artichoke Dip

Use Asiago cheese in place of Parmesan. Omit spinach and Cheddar. Add 2 chopped roasted red bell peppers (page 161) with artichokes.

• *Slow Cooker Size: 3 1/2 to 6 qt*

2	cloves garlic, minced	2
2	8-oz (250 g) packages cream cheese, softened	2
1/4 cup	mayonnaise	50 mL
1/3 cup	grated Parmesan cheese	75 mL
1	10-oz (300 g) package frozen chopped spinach, defrosted and squeezed dry	1
1	14-oz (398 mL) can artichoke hearts, rinsed, drained and coarsely chopped	1
2/3 cup	grated Cheddar cheese	150 mL

1. In a food processor or bowl, combine garlic, cream cheese, mayonnaise and Parmesan. Process until smooth and creamy.
2. Add spinach and artichokes and combine. Spoon mixture into slow cooker stoneware.
3. Cover and cook on **Low** for 2 to 3 hours or on **High** for 1 1/2 to 2 hours, or until heated through.
4. Sprinkle with Cheddar, cover and cook on **High** for 15 to 20 minutes, or until cheese melts.

Hot Corn Dip

**Makes about
6 cups (1.5 L)**

The inspiration for
this recipe hails from
the Deep South. The
jalapeño pepper adds
a definite spicy nip.

There are a variety
of pre-shredded
cheeses available in
the supermarket.
If you wish, you can
substitute a Mexican
blend or hot pepper
Monterey Jack in
place of the Cheddar.

Enjoy with tortilla chips
and a Mexican beer.

- *Slow Cooker Size: 3 1/2 to 4 qt*

1 tbsp	butter	15 mL
3 1/2 cups	fresh or frozen and defrosted corn kernels	875 mL
1	onion, finely chopped	1
1/2 tsp	salt	2 mL
1/4 tsp	black pepper	1 mL
2	cloves garlic, minced	2
1	green onion, finely chopped	1
1	jalapeño pepper, seeded and finely chopped	1
1/2	red bell pepper, seeded and finely chopped	1/2
1 cup	mayonnaise	250 mL
1 1/2 cups	grated Cheddar cheese	375 mL

1. In a large nonstick skillet, melt butter over medium-high heat. Add corn, onion, salt and pepper. Cook, stirring occasionally, until kernels turn a deep golden brown, about 5 minutes. Transfer to a bowl.

2. Add garlic, green onion, jalapeño, red pepper, mayonnaise and cheese to corn. Mix well. Spoon into lightly greased slow cooker stoneware.

3. Cover and cook on **Low** for 3 to 4 hours or on **High** for 1 to 2 hours, or until bubbly. Serve hot.

> **Handling Hot Peppers**
>
> When chopping and seeding jalapeños or other hot peppers, make sure you keep your hands away from your eyes. Better yet, wear rubber or latex gloves and wash your hands, cutting board and utensils thoroughly in hot soapy water after handling peppers.

Nacho Cheese Dip

Makes about 4 cups (1 L)

This dip is sure to be a hit during football playoffs; serve it with lots of tortilla chips for scooping.

While many North Americans prefer Cheddar cheese, the key to this creamy dip is the processed cheese loaf, which will not curdle when heated. Enjoy the indulgence!

• *Slow Cooker Size: 3 1/2 to 6 qt*

½ cup	beer	125 mL
1 tsp	ground cumin	5 mL
½ tsp	dried oregano leaves	2 mL
½ tsp	garlic powder	2 mL
1	14-oz (398 mL) can refried beans	1
½ cup	salsa	125 mL
1	1-lb (500 g) processed cheese loaf, cut in ½-inch (1 cm) cubes	1
¼ cup	chopped fresh cilantro	50 mL

1. In a small saucepan, combine beer, cumin, oregano and garlic powder. Bring to a boil, reduce heat and simmer for 2 minutes.

2. In a bowl, combine beans, salsa, cheese cubes and beer mixture. Spoon into lightly greased slow cooker stoneware.

3. Cover and cook on **Low** for 3 to 4 hours or on **High** for 1 to 2 hours, or until bubbly and cheese has melted. Sprinkle with cilantro.

Bourbon Bangers

Makes 10 to 12 appetizer servings

Sometimes a party just doesn't seem like a party without cocktail franks. Serve them straight from the slow cooker with lots of napkins or small plates to catch the drips.

This recipe can easily be doubled and made in a large slow cooker.

• *Slow Cooker Size: 3 1/2 qt*

1 1/4 cups	ketchup	300 mL
1/2 cup	packed brown sugar	125 mL
1	small onion, finely chopped	1
2 tsp	prepared mustard	10 mL
1/4 cup	Bourbon whiskey or orange juice	50 mL
1 lb	smoked cocktail sausages, separated if attached	500 g

1. In a bowl, combine ketchup, brown sugar, onion, mustard and Bourbon.

2. Place sausages in slow cooker stoneware and pour sauce over top.

3. Cover and cook on **Low** for 3 to 4 hours, or until sauce is hot and sausages are heated through.

Fruity Glazed Meatballs

Makes 10 to 12 appetizer servings (about 30 meatballs)

People just can't seem to get enough of this slow cooker party classic with its tangy sweet and sour sauce.

If you are short of time, you can make the meatballs ahead or substitute storebought precooked frozen meatballs. Defrost for about 30 minutes at room temperature before adding them to the slow cooker.

Make Ahead
Meatballs can be made ahead and frozen. Bake meatballs, allow to cool and then freeze for up to a month. Before adding to slow cooker, allow meatballs to defrost for about 30 minutes at room temperature.

• Slow Cooker Size: 3½ qt

1 lb	lean ground pork, turkey or chicken	500 g
1	egg, lightly beaten	1
½ cup	dry bread crumbs	125 mL
3 tbsp	finely chopped fresh parsley	45 mL
2	green onions, finely chopped	2
1 tsp	soy sauce	5 mL
½ tsp	salt	2 mL
¼ tsp	black pepper	1 mL

GRAPE CHILI SAUCE

1 cup	chili sauce	250 mL
1 cup	grape jelly	250 mL
1 tsp	lemon juice	5 mL
2 tbsp	packed brown sugar	25 mL
1 tbsp	soy sauce	15 mL

1. To make meatballs, in a large bowl, combine ground pork, egg, bread crumbs, parsley, green onions, soy sauce, salt and pepper. Mix well and shape into 1-inch (2.5 cm) balls.

2. Arrange meatballs on a foil-lined baking sheet in a single layer and bake in a preheated 400°F (200°C) oven for 10 to 12 minutes, or until no longer pink inside.

3. To prepare sauce, combine chili sauce, grape jelly, lemon juice, brown sugar and soy sauce in slow cooker stoneware. Add meatballs.

4. Cover and cook on **High** for 3 to 4 hours, or until sauce is bubbly and meatballs are hot.

Toasting Sesame Seeds

To toast sesame seeds, spread on a baking sheet and bake in a preheated 350°F (180°C) oven for 4 minutes, or until golden. Or place seeds in a dry skillet over medium-high heat and cook, stirring, for 4 to 6 minutes, or until golden.

Turkish Winglets

Makes 4 to 6 appetizer servings

These Middle Eastern inspired chicken wings, smothered in a tasty mixture of chutney and spices, are finger-licking good. You may want to serve them as a main course with steamed rice (page 73) and green beans.

Try to buy extra-large chicken wings that have already been separated at the joint. They are perfect for these appetizers as they are exceptionally meaty. Broiling the wings before slow cooking helps to remove excess fat from the skin.

• *Slow Cooker Size: 3 1/2 to 6 qt*

1/3 cup	mango chutney	75 mL
1 tbsp	liquid honey	15 mL
1 tbsp	lime juice	15 mL
2 tsp	Dijon mustard	10 mL
1 1/2 tsp	grated gingerroot	7 mL
1/4 tsp	five-spice powder	1 mL
2 lbs	chicken wings, tips removed, split in half	1 kg

TOPPING (OPTIONAL)

1 tbsp	chopped fresh parsley	15 mL
1 tbsp	sesame seeds, toasted (page 26)	15 mL
2 tsp	grated orange zest	10 mL

1. Chop any large pieces of fruit in chutney. In a small bowl, combine chutney, honey, lime juice, mustard, gingerroot and five-spice powder.

2. Arrange chicken wings on a foil-lined baking sheet in a single layer. Broil under preheated broiler 6 inches (15 cm) from heat for 15 to 20 minutes, or until golden. Turn wings once during cooking.

3. Discard drippings and transfer wings to slow cooker stoneware. Pour reserved sauce over wings.

4. Cover and cook on **Low** for 3 to 4 hours, or until wings are glazed and no longer pink inside. Turn twice during cooking time.

5. Prepare topping if using. In a small bowl, combine parsley, sesame seeds and orange zest. Sprinkle wings with parsley mixture before serving.

Five-Spice Powder

Five-spice powder is a common Asian seasoning. You can find it at any Asian supermarket or spice store. You can also make your own by combining equal parts ground cinnamon, cloves, fennel seeds, star anise and Szechwan peppercorns.

Sun-dried Tomato Appetizer Cheesecake

Makes 8 to 10 appetizer servings

Holiday entertaining just got easier! This fabulous savory cheesecake can be made the day before your party. You will need to use a large round or oval slow cooker. Make sure your slow cooker is big enough to hold the springform pan. (For tips on using a springform pan in the slow cooker, see page 14.)

Cheesecakes cook beautifully in the slow cooker. Because of the moist heat, cracks do not appear and a silky top is the result.

For an added touch, you can sprinkle chopped toasted pine nuts (page 162) over the cooked cheesecake.

• Slow Cooker Size: 5 to 7 qt

³⁄₄ cup	crushed buttery-type cracker crumbs	175 mL
3 tbsp	butter, melted	45 mL
2	8-oz (250 g) packages cream cheese, softened	2
1 tbsp	sun-dried tomato oil or olive oil	15 mL
2	eggs, lightly beaten	2
¹⁄₄ cup	whipping (35%) cream	50 mL
³⁄₄ cup	grated Havarti cheese	175 mL
¹⁄₄ cup	sliced oil-packed sun-dried tomatoes, well drained	50 mL
4	green onions, chopped	4
¹⁄₂ tsp	dried rosemary leaves, crumbled	2 mL

1. To make crust, in a bowl, combine cracker crumbs and melted butter. Press mixture into bottom of a well-greased 7- or 8-inch (17 or 20 cm) springform pan (or another pan that will fit in slow cooker). Place in freezer until ready to use.

2. To make filling, in a large bowl, using an electric mixer, beat cream cheese and oil until smooth. Beat in eggs one at a time until incorporated. Beat in whipping cream.

3. Gently fold in Havarti, sun-dried tomatoes, green onions and rosemary.

4. Spoon filling over prepared crust and wrap entire pan tightly with foil, securing with string or elastic bands.

5. Place pan in slow cooker stoneware lined with cheesecloth or foil strips (page 14). Pour in enough boiling water to come 1 inch (2.5 cm) up sides of springform pan (if pan fits snugly in slow cooker, you can add water before inserting pan).

6. Cover and cook on **High** for 3 to 4 hours, or until edges are set and center is just slightly jiggly. Remove pan from slow cooker and chill for 2 hours or up to overnight in refrigerator.

Olives in Red Wine

Black olives absorb the flavor of red wine and fennel in this warm appetizer. Be sure to provide toothpicks as well as a dish for the olive pits.

A mini (1 qt) slow cooker is ideal for this recipe. It's just the right size and will keep the olives at the right temperature.

Buy Kalamata olives if you can find them. They are assertively flavored ripe Greek olives marinated in wine vinegar or olive oil. Be sure to use the brine-cured variety in this recipe.

• *Slow Cooker Size: 1 to 3$\frac{1}{2}$ qt*

1 cup	unpitted brine-cured black olives	250 mL
$\frac{1}{2}$ cup	dry red wine	125 mL
$\frac{1}{4}$ tsp	fennel seeds, coarsely crushed	1 mL
1	clove garlic, peeled and thinly sliced	1
2 tsp	olive oil	10 mL

1. Combine olives, wine, fennel seeds, garlic and olive oil in slow cooker stoneware

2. Cover and cook on **Low** for 3 to 4 hours, or until olives are heated through. Serve warm.

Best Beer Nuts

Makes about 2½ cups (625 mL)

Who would have thought that these favorite stadium nibblers could be made in the slow cooker? You won't believe the rave reviews you will get, and the cleanup is a lot easier than making them in the oven. Of course, drinking a beer with them is a must!

Keep these delicious nuts on hand as extra nibbles for parties. They will keep in an airtight container at room temperature for up to a month. They also make a perfect hostess gift packaged in an attractive container with ribbon tied around it.

• *Slow Cooker Size: 3½ to 6 qt*

1 cup	granulated sugar	250 mL
¼ cup	water	50 mL
2 cups	peanuts, preferably unsalted	500 mL

1. In a small bowl, combine sugar and water.

2. Place peanuts in slow cooker stoneware. Pour sugar mixture over nuts and toss to coat.

3. Cover and cook on **High**, stirring frequently, for 2 to 3 hours, or until sugar mixture is golden brown and peanuts are toasted. Turn out onto a foil-lined baking sheet and set aside to cool.

Chocolate Chai Tea

Makes 10 to 12 servings

Chai is an Indian spiced tea that can be enjoyed hot or cold. Here it is mixed with cocoa to make a very creamy spiced hot chocolate — perfect after a day of outdoor winter activities. Ladle the tea into mugs and serve garnished with a cinnamon stick.

For added orange flavor, float a long strip of orange zest in the tea mix while it is in the slow cooker. Remove before serving so it doesn't impart a bitter aftertaste.

For a more authentic flavor, brew tea with black tea leaves such as Darjeeling. Strain before adding to the slow cooker.

• Slow Cooker Size: 3 1/2 to 6 qt

1 3/4 cups	skim milk powder	425 mL
3/4 cup	powdered non-dairy creamer	175 mL
3/4 cup	granulated sugar	175 mL
1/2 cup	unsweetened cocoa powder	125 mL
2 tsp	ground cinnamon	10 mL
1 tsp	ground nutmeg	5 mL
12 cups	brewed black tea	3 L

1. In a bowl, combine skim milk powder, powdered creamer, sugar, cocoa, cinnamon and nutmeg.

2. Transfer mixture to slow cooker stoneware. Slowly whisk in tea until mixture is smooth and no lumps remain.

3. Cover and cook on **Low** for 4 to 5 hours, or until hot. Stir well before serving.

Mulled Raspberry Tea

Makes 6 servings

This beautiful lemony ruby-red drink sparkles and tastes delicious. Serve it at winter gatherings. The recipe can easily be doubled and cooked in a large slow cooker. Double all ingredients except for the raspberries.

• Slow Cooker Size: $3\frac{1}{2}$ to 6 qt

3	whole allspice berries	3
I	cinnamon stick	I
I tsp	whole cloves	5 mL
2 cups	brewed black tea	500 mL
2 cups	cranberry raspberry cocktail	500 mL
I cup	frozen lemonade concentrate	250 mL
$\frac{1}{2}$ cup	water	125 mL
I	$13\frac{1}{2}$-oz (400 g) package frozen raspberries in syrup, defrosted	I

1. Wrap allspice, cinnamon stick and cloves in a double thickness of cheesecloth and tie with kitchen twine to form a bag.

2. Combine tea, cranberry raspberry cocktail, lemonade concentrate, water and raspberries in slow cooker stoneware. Add spice bag.

3. Cover and cook on **Low** for 2 to 5 hours, or until hot and fragrant. Remove spice bag before serving.

Fruity Glazed Meatballs (page 26)

Soups

∿∿∿∿∿∿∿∿∿∿∿∿∿∿∿∿∿

Italian Sausage and Tortellini Soup (page 39)

Cabbage Roll Soup

This cabbage roll soup
is hearty enough to be a
meal by itself — perfect
for warding off winter's
chill. Garnish each
serving with a dollop
of sour cream.

Look for a small
cabbage for this soup
or, to save time, buy
packaged pre-shredded
coleslaw cabbage.

There is no need to
pre-cook the rice in this
recipe. As the meatballs
simmer in the broth,
the liquid cooks the
rice, resulting in a
tender, tasty meatball.

Make an extra batch of
meatballs to have on
hand for the next time
you want to make
this soup. They freeze
well and will keep in
the freezer for up
to one month.

• *Slow Cooker Size: 5 to 6 qt*

½ lb	lean ground beef	250 g
½ lb	lean ground pork	250 g
1	egg, lightly beaten	1
¾ cup	uncooked long-grain parboiled white rice	175 mL
1	small onion, finely chopped	1
2	cloves garlic, minced	2
½ tsp	salt	2 mL
¼ tsp	black pepper	1 mL
3 cups	chicken stock	750 mL
1	28-oz (796 mL) can tomatoes, chopped, with juices	1
1	10-oz (284 mL) can condensed tomato soup, undiluted	1
4 cups	shredded cabbage	1 L
¼ cup	chopped fresh parsley	50 mL

1. In a bowl, combine ground beef, ground pork, egg,
rice, onion, garlic, salt and pepper. Shape into
1-inch (2.5 cm) balls.

2. Arrange meatballs on a foil-lined baking sheet and bake
in a preheated 350°F (180°C) oven for 20 minutes,
or until browned and no longer pink inside.

3. In slow cooker stoneware, combine stock, tomatoes,
tomato soup and cabbage. Add meatballs and stir
gently to combine.

4. Cover and cook on **Low** for 8 to 10 hours or on
High for 4 to 6 hours, or until hot and bubbling.
Stir in parsley.

Cheesy Salmon Chowder

Makes 4 to 6 servings

My family are big fish eaters, and salmon is their favorite. This hearty chowder is one they ask for again and again. It can be made using fresh, canned or smoked salmon. If you are using canned salmon, be sure to remove the dark skin and large bones first.

You can replace the evaporated milk with 1½ cups (375 mL) cream if you wish.

• Slow Cooker Size: 3½ to 6 qt

1	large onion, chopped	1
3	potatoes, peeled and cut in ½-inch (1 cm) cubes	3
1	large carrot, peeled and finely chopped	1
1	stalk celery, finely chopped	1
1	clove garlic, minced	1
¼ cup	uncooked long-grain parboiled white rice	50 mL
3 cups	chicken or vegetable stock	750 mL
¾ tsp	salt	4 mL
½ tsp	dried thyme leaves	2 mL
¼ tsp	black pepper	1 mL
1 cup	flaked cooked salmon	250 mL
1	13-oz (385 mL) can evaporated milk	1
1 cup	grated Cheddar cheese	250 mL

1. Combine onion, potatoes, carrot, celery, garlic, rice, stock, salt, thyme and pepper in slow cooker stoneware. Cover and cook on **Low** for 8 to 10 hours, or until vegetables and rice are tender.

2. Stir in salmon, milk and cheese. Cover and cook on **High** for 15 minutes, or until salmon is heated through.

Dutch Farmer Bean Soup

Makes 4 to 6 servings

Pureeing some of the soup gives this dish body. Serve it with coleslaw (page 57) with added chopped apples and raisins, accompanied by slices of warm pumpernickel bread.

Baby carrots work well in soups. They are already peeled, which eliminates an extra step.

Add the smoked sausages at the end, just to warm through. Since they are already cooked, the skin will toughen if the sausages are left in the soup too long. If you can't find turkey kielbasa, any smoked pork sausage will work.

• *Slow Cooker Size: 3 1/2 to 6 qt*

1 cup	baby carrots	250 mL
1	onion, chopped	1
2	cloves garlic, minced	2
4 cups	chicken stock	1 L
1 tsp	dried Italian herb seasoning	5 mL
2	19-oz (540 mL) cans Great Northern or white kidney beans, rinsed and drained, or 4 cups (1 L) home-cooked white beans (page 145)	2
4	smoked turkey kielbasa sausages, halved lengthwise and cut in 1/2-inch (1 cm) pieces	4
2 cups	fresh baby spinach leaves	500 mL

1. Combine carrots, onion, garlic, stock, Italian seasoning and beans in slow cooker stoneware.

2. Cover and cook on **Low** for 6 to 10 hours or on **High** for 3 to 4 hours, or until vegetables are tender and soup is bubbling.

3. Transfer 2 cups (500 mL) soup to a blender or food processor and blend until smooth. Return pureed mixture to slow cooker and add kielbasa and spinach. Cover and cook on **High** for 15 to 20 minutes, or until spinach is wilted and kielbasa is heated through.

Dried Italian Herb Seasoning

If you don't have a dried Italian herb seasoning mix, use a combination of basil, marjoram, thyme and oregano. Instead of 1 tsp (5 mL) Italian seasoning, use 1/2 tsp (2 mL) dried basil leaves, 1/4 tsp (1 mL) dried marjoram leaves, 1/4 tsp (1 mL) dried thyme leaves and 1/4 tsp (1 mL) dried oregano leaves.

Easy Wieners and Beaners Soup

Makes 4 to 6 servings

This nutrition-packed soup is a sure-fire way to get the kids to eat their vegetables! Try sprinkling a little grated mozzarella cheese on top. Kids love the way it "strings" when they spoon into it.

I like to buy veal wieners in the deli department of the supermarket to use in this recipe instead of the pre-packaged hot-dog wieners.

If your family is not fond of vegetable cocktail juice, substitute tomato juice.

Using beans in tomato sauce with added maple syrup adds a little sweetness to the recipe, but you can substitute any canned baked beans. (Baked beans in barbecue sauce will add a spicy punch!)

• *Slow Cooker Size: 3½ to 6 qt*

4 cups	tomato vegetable cocktail juice	1 L
2	14-oz (398 mL) cans baked beans in tomato sauce with maple syrup	2
3	carrots, peeled and finely chopped	3
1	small onion, finely chopped	1
1	clove garlic, minced	1
½ cup	fresh or frozen and defrosted corn kernels	125 mL
1 tsp	Worcestershire sauce	5 mL
½ tsp	dry mustard	2 mL
1	bay leaf	1
4 to 6	wieners or hot dogs, cut in ½-inch (1 cm) pieces	4 to 6
	Salt and black pepper to taste	

1. Combine vegetable juice, beans, carrots, onion, garlic, corn, Worcestershire, mustard and bay leaf in slow cooker stoneware.

2. Cover and cook on **Low** for 6 to 10 hours or on **High** for 3 to 4 hours, or until carrots are tender.

3. Add wieners and cook on **High** for 20 to 30 minutes, or until heated through. Discard bay leaf and season soup with salt and pepper.

French Onion Soup

Makes 6 servings

In restaurants, bowls of onion soup are served capped with toasted French bread sprinkled with cheese and broiled to melt the cheese. For this version, broil the cheese on the bread first, then place in the bottom of the serving bowls.

Aside from using sweet onions, the key to making a great onion soup is the stock (page 43). Use the best-quality stock you can.

• *Slow Cooker Size: 3 1/2 to 6 qt*

1/4 cup	butter	50 mL
4	large sweet onions, sliced	4
2	cloves garlic, minced	2
2 tbsp	all-purpose flour	25 mL
6 cups	beef stock	1.5 L
1/4 cup	dry sherry or dry red wine	50 mL
1 tbsp	Worcestershire sauce	15 mL
1 tsp	granulated sugar	5 mL
1/2 tsp	salt	2 mL
1/4 tsp	dried thyme leaves	1 mL
1	bay leaf	1
1/2 tsp	black pepper	2 mL

CROUTONS

6	slices French bread (1/2 inch/1 cm thick)	6
1 cup	grated Swiss cheese	250 mL

1. Combine butter, onions and garlic in slow cooker stoneware. Cover and cook on **High** for 40 to 60 minutes, or until onions begin to brown slightly around edges.

2. Sprinkle onions with flour and stir to combine. Add stock, sherry, Worcestershire, sugar, salt, thyme, bay leaf and pepper.

3. Cover and cook on **Low** for 6 to 8 hours or on **High** for 3 to 4 hours, or until onions are tender and soup is bubbling. Discard bay leaf.

4. To make croutons, place bread slices on a baking sheet. Place under preheated broiler about 6 inches (15 cm) from the element and broil for about 2 minutes, or until browned. Turn bread, sprinkle with cheese and continue to broil until cheese is bubbling, about 1 minute.

5. Place bread croutons in bottom of individual serving bowls and spoon soup over top.

Italian Sausage and Tortellini Soup

Makes 4 to 6 servings

Serve this soup after a football game, accompanied by big bowls of chips and dip.

Italian sausage is highly seasoned and adds a wallop of great flavor. For less heat, stick to the mild variety.

• *Slow Cooker Size: 3 1/2 to 6 qt*

1 lb	mild or hot Italian sausages, casings removed	500 g
1	large onion, chopped	1
2	carrots, peeled and chopped	2
4 cups	beef or chicken stock	1 L
1/2 tsp	dried Italian herb seasoning (page 36)	2 mL
1/2 tsp	salt	2 mL
1/4 tsp	black pepper	1 mL
1	7 1/2-oz (213 mL) can tomato sauce	1
1	19-oz (540 mL) can tomatoes, chopped, with juices	1
2 cups	sliced mushrooms	500 mL
1	10-oz (300 g) package fresh or frozen cheese-filled tortellini	1
1	zucchini, quartered lengthwise and sliced	1
1/4 cup	chopped fresh parsley	50 mL
2 tbsp	grated Parmesan cheese	25 mL

1. In a large nonstick skillet over medium-high heat, cook sausage meat for 8 to 10 minutes, or until browned, stirring to break up meat. With a slotted spoon, transfer to slow cooker stoneware.

2. Add onion, carrots, stock, Italian seasoning, salt, pepper, tomato sauce, tomatoes and mushrooms to slow cooker.

3. Cover and cook on **Low** for 6 to 10 hours or on **High** for 3 to 4 hours, or until vegetables are tender.

4. Meanwhile, cook tortellini according to package directions. Drain.

5. Add zucchini, parsley and tortellini to slow cooker and cook on **High** for 15 to 20 minutes, or until heated through and zucchini is tender.

6. Spoon into individual bowls and top with grated Parmesan cheese.

Mulligatawny Soup

Makes 6 to 8 servings

This famous Indian soup was originally developed by cooks who served in English homes during the colonization of India in the eighteenth century. It is based on chicken and vegetables cooked in a rich stock that has been seasoned with curry. Serve topped with toasted shredded coconut if you wish. For a heartier meal, serve it over steamed basmati rice (page 73).

• *Slow Cooker Size: 3 1/2 to 6 qt*

1 tbsp	all-purpose flour	15 mL
1 lb	boneless skinless chicken thighs, cut in 1-inch (2.5 cm) pieces	500 g
1 tbsp	vegetable oil	15 mL
1 tbsp	curry powder	15 mL
1 tsp	ground ginger	5 mL
1/2 tsp	hot red pepper flakes	2 mL
1/4 tsp	ground cloves	1 mL
4 cups	chicken stock, divided	1 L
2	carrots, peeled and finely chopped	2
1	onion, finely chopped	1
2	stalks celery, finely chopped	2
2	cloves garlic, minced	2
1/2 cup	diced turnip	125 mL
1	Granny Smith apple, unpeeled, chopped	1
1	19-oz (540 mL) can chickpeas, rinsed and drained, or 2 cups (500 mL) home-cooked chickpeas (page 145)	1
1 tbsp	grated lemon zest	15 mL
	Juice of 1 lemon	
1 tbsp	chopped fresh cilantro	15 mL

1. Place flour in a large heavy-duty plastic bag. In batches, toss chicken in flour to coat.

2. In a large nonstick skillet, heat oil over medium-high heat. Add chicken, curry powder, ginger, hot pepper flakes and cloves. Cook, stirring occasionally, for 5 to 7 minutes, or until chicken is browned on all sides. With a slotted spoon, transfer chicken to slow cooker stoneware.

3. Add 1 cup (250 mL) stock to skillet. Bring to a boil and stir to scrape up any brown bits. Transfer stock mixture to slow cooker.

4. Add carrots, onion, celery, garlic, turnip, apple, chickpeas and remaining stock to slow cooker. Mix well to combine.

5. Cover and cook on **Low** for 6 to 8 hours or on **High** for 3 to 4 hours, or until vegetables are tender and soup is bubbling.

6. Stir in lemon zest, lemon juice and cilantro.

Curry Powder

Curry powder, a blend of more than twenty herbs, seeds and spices, is integral to Indian cuisine (in India, most cooks blend their own mixtures). Cardamom, chilies, cinnamon, coriander, cumin, fennel, mace, pepper, poppy and sesame seeds and saffron are common curry seasonings. Turmeric gives curry its distinctive yellow color.

Curry paste can be used instead of curry powder. It comes in different heat levels, so buy a mild version if you don't like your curry too hot.

To eliminate the raw taste of curry powder and sweeten the spice, sauté it in a dry skillet before using. Cook for about 30 seconds, or just until fragrant.

Meaty Minestrone

**Makes 6 to
8 servings**

Minestrone means
"big soup" in Italian and
refers to a thick soup
full of vegetables and
pasta. This meaty
version makes a
hearty meal.

When you purchase a
piece of real Parmesan
cheese (e.g., Parmigiano
Reggiano), it usually
comes with the rind.
The rind is too tough
to grate or eat, so add
it to this soup for
extra flavor. (Be sure
to discard it before
serving the soup.)

• *Slow Cooker Size: 5 to 6 qt*

1 tbsp	vegetable oil	15 mL
1 lb	stewing beef, cut in 1-inch (2.5 cm) cubes	500 g
¾ tsp	dried Italian herb seasoning (page 36)	4 mL
1 tsp	salt	5 mL
½ tsp	black pepper	2 mL
3 cups	beef stock, divided	750 mL
1	19-oz (540 mL) can tomatoes, chopped, with juices	1
2	cloves garlic, minced	2
2	carrots, peeled and finely chopped	2
1	stalk celery, finely chopped	1
1 cup	shredded cabbage	250 mL
1	bay leaf	1
1	12-oz (355 mL) can cola	1
1	19-oz (540 mL) can white kidney beans, rinsed and drained, or 2 cups (500 mL) home-cooked beans (page 145)	1
1	1-inch (2.5 cm) piece Parmesan cheese rind	1
1 cup	diced green beans	250 mL
1	small zucchini, cut in half lengthwise and chopped	1
1 cup	cooked macaroni or other small pasta	250 mL
2 tbsp	grated Parmesan cheese	25 mL

1. In a large nonstick skillet, heat oil over medium-high heat. Add beef cubes, Italian seasoning, salt and pepper and cook, stirring, for 8 to 10 minutes, or until meat is browned on all sides. With a slotted spoon, transfer meat to slow cooker stoneware.

2. Add 1 cup (250 mL) stock to skillet and bring to a boil, scraping up any browned bits from bottom of pan. Add to meat in slow cooker.

3. Add remaining stock, tomatoes, garlic, carrots, celery, cabbage, bay leaf, cola and kidney beans to slow cooker. Stir to combine. Immerse Parmesan cheese wedge in soup mixture.

4. Cover and cook on **Low** for 8 to 10 hours or on **High** for 4 to 6 hours, or until meat and vegetables are tender and soup is bubbling.

5. Stir in green beans, zucchini and macaroni.

6. Cover and cook on **High** for 20 to 25 minutes, or until hot and bubbly. Discard Parmesan rind and bay leaf.

7. Spoon soup into individual bowls and sprinkle with grated Parmesan cheese.

Stock

Stock refers to the strained liquid that results from cooking poultry, meat or vegetables and seasonings in water. Other terms for this include broth and bouillon. The best stock is homemade, but if time won't allow, use canned stock (dilute as directed) or refrigerated stocks sold in Tetra Paks. Try to avoid using bouillon powder or cubes since these tend to be quite salty and don't give the same rich taste. If you do use powdered stock or cubes, add salt to taste at the end of the cooking.

Mexican Squash Soup

**Makes 6 to
8 servings**

This easy-to-make soup is fun for a party because the guests can help themselves to a variety of colorful garnishes. Along with the toppings, be sure to pass a basket of tortilla chips.

Make Ahead

This soup can be prepared up to 24 hours before cooking. Combine ingredients in slow cooker stoneware and refrigerate overnight. The next day, place stoneware in slow cooker and continue to cook as directed.

• *Slow Cooker Size: $3\frac{1}{2}$ to 6 qt*

2	onions, finely chopped	2
2	cloves garlic, minced	2
4 cups	diced squash	1 L
1 tsp	ground cumin	5 mL
1 tsp	salt	5 mL
$\frac{1}{2}$ tsp	dried oregano leaves	2 mL
$\frac{1}{2}$ tsp	hot red pepper flakes	2 mL
$\frac{1}{2}$ tsp	black pepper	2 mL
4 cups	vegetable or chicken stock	1 L
3 cups	fresh or frozen and defrosted corn kernels	750 mL
$\frac{1}{2}$	red bell pepper, seeded and finely chopped	$\frac{1}{2}$
$\frac{1}{2}$ cup	chopped fresh cilantro	125 mL

TOPPINGS

$\frac{1}{2}$ cup	grated Cheddar or Monterey Jack cheese	125 mL
$\frac{1}{2}$ cup	pine nuts, toasted (page 151)	125 mL
$\frac{1}{2}$ cup	walnut halves, toasted (page 151)	125 mL
2	jalapeño peppers, seeded and chopped	2

1. Combine onions, garlic, squash, cumin, salt, oregano, hot pepper flakes, pepper and stock in slow cooker stoneware.

2. Cover and cook on **Low** for 8 to 10 hours or on **High** for 4 to 6 hours, or until vegetables are tender and soup is bubbling.

3. Stir in corn, red pepper and cilantro.

4. Cover and cook on **High** for 15 to 20 minutes, or until heated through.

5. Spoon into individual bowls and sprinkle with cheese, pine nuts, walnuts and jalapeños.

Old World Bean and Beer Soup

Makes 4 to 6 servings

This homey soup is reminiscent of a European-style vegetable soup. Serve lots of extra pretzels to nibble on.

For company, serve this soup with a platter of cheeses such as Cheddar, Swiss, Gouda and Jarlsberg. Label the cheeses and arrange them on a platter with grapes and slices of marbled rye and pumpernickel bread.

Open the beer and set out the night before making the soup to allow it to go flat.

Make Ahead

This soup can be assembled up to 24 hours before cooking. Combine ingredients in slow cooker stoneware and refrigerate overnight. The next day, place stoneware in slow cooker and continue to cook as directed.

• Slow Cooker Size: 3½ to 6 qt

1	large onion, finely chopped	1
2	carrots, peeled and chopped	2
2	stalks celery, finely chopped	2
2	cloves garlic, minced	2
4 cups	chicken stock	1 L
1	12-oz (341 mL) can or bottle dark beer, flat	1
1 tsp	Worcestershire sauce	5 mL
1 tsp	dried thyme leaves	5 mL
½ tsp	dried marjoram leaves	2 mL
½ tsp	hot red pepper flakes	2 mL
1 tsp	salt	5 mL
½ tsp	black pepper	2 mL
2	19-oz (540 mL) can white pea (navy) beans, rinsed and drained, or 4 cups (1 L) home-cooked beans (page 145)	2
2 cups	chopped cooked ham	500 mL
¼ cup	chopped fresh parsley	50 mL
2 tbsp	crushed pretzels	25 mL
2 tbsp	chopped green onions	25 mL

1. Combine onion, carrots, celery, garlic, stock, beer, Worcestershire sauce, thyme, marjoram, hot pepper flakes, salt, pepper, beans and ham in slow cooker stoneware. Stir to combine.

2. Cover and cook on **Low** for 6 to 10 hours or on **High** for 3 to 4 hours, or until vegetables are tender and soup is bubbling. Stir in parsley.

3. Spoon into individual serving bowls and sprinkle with crushed pretzels and green onions.

Roasted Pear and Parsnip Soup

Makes 4 to 6 servings

Parsnips "roasted" in the slow cooker give a smoky taste to this hearty winter soup. Serve it garnished with fresh thyme sprigs.

The best pears to choose for this soup are Bartlett or Bosc.

Make Ahead
This soup can be prepared up to the puree and then refrigerated or frozen. Defrost puree before placing in slow cooker.

• *Slow Cooker Size: 3$\frac{1}{2}$ to 6 qt*

2 cups	chopped peeled parsnips	500 mL
1	nearly ripe pear, peeled and chopped	1
1	onion, chopped	1
2	cloves garlic, minced	2
1	yellow bell pepper, seeded and chopped	1
1 tbsp	butter, melted	15 mL
1 tbsp	packed brown sugar	15 mL
1 tbsp	balsamic vinegar	15 mL
$\frac{1}{2}$ tsp	dried thyme leaves	2 mL
4 cups	vegetable or chicken stock, divided	1 L

1. Place parsnips, pear, onion, garlic and yellow pepper in slow cooker stoneware.

2. In a small bowl, combine melted butter, brown sugar, vinegar and thyme. Pour over vegetables and toss to coat.

3. Cover and cook on **Low** for 4 to 6 hours or on **High** for 2 to 3 hours, or until vegetables are tender.

4. In a blender or food processor, puree vegetable mixture with 1 cup (250 mL) stock until smooth. Return mixture to slow cooker and add remaining stock.

5. Cover and cook on **Low** for 4 to 6 hours or on **High** for 3 to 4 hours, or until bubbling.

Southwestern Pumpkin Soup

**Makes 4 to
6 servings**

This easy-to-make soup
is flavored with cumin
and chili powder. Make
sure you buy a can of
pumpkin puree, not
pumpkin pie filling.

• *Slow Cooker Size: 3 1/2 to 6 qt*

3 cups	vegetable or chicken stock	750 mL
1	28-oz (796 mL) can pumpkin puree	1
1 tbsp	packed brown sugar	15 mL
1 tsp	ground cumin	5 mL
1/2 tsp	chili powder	2 mL
Pinch	ground nutmeg	Pinch
1	14-oz (400 mL) can coconut milk	1
1/2 tsp	grated lime zest	2 mL
2 tsp	lime juice	10 mL
1/2 cup	grated Cheddar cheese	125 mL
1 tbsp	chopped fresh cilantro	15 mL

1. Combine stock, pumpkin puree, brown sugar, cumin, chili powder and nutmeg in slow cooker stoneware.

2. Cover and cook on **Low** for 4 to 6 hours or on **High** for 2 to 3 hours, or until hot and bubbling.

3. Stir in coconut milk, lime zest and juice. Spoon soup into individual serving bowls and top with grated Cheddar and cilantro.

Coconut Milk

Canned coconut milk is made from grated and soaked coconut pulp, not (as you might expect) from the liquid inside the coconut. It can be found in the Asian or canned milk section of most supermarkets or in Asian food stores. Make sure you don't buy coconut cream, which is used to make tropical drinks such as piña coladas.

Spicy Sweet Potato Soup

Makes 6 servings

See if your guests can guess the secret ingredient in this soup (peanut butter).

Be sure to grate the zest before juicing the lime when you are preparing the ingredients for this recipe.

An immersion blender is ideal for pureeing the soup right in the slow cooker without having to transfer it to a blender or food processor.

This soup's exotic flavors suit a spicy wine such as a Gewürztraminer. Serve it with crusty European-style bread.

Make Ahead
The puree can be prepared in advance (up to the end of Step 3) and refrigerated for up to three days or frozen for up to one month. Reheat puree with remaining stock in a saucepan on the stove.

• Slow Cooker Size: 3 1/2 to 6 qt

2	large sweet potatoes, peeled and chopped (about 1 1/2 to 2 lbs/750 g to 1 kg)	2
1	onion, chopped	1
2	cloves garlic, peeled and sliced	2
4 cups	vegetable or chicken stock	1 L
1/2 tsp	ground cumin	2 mL
1/4 tsp	hot red pepper flakes	1 mL
1 tsp	ground ginger	5 mL
1/4 cup	crunchy or smooth peanut butter	50 mL
	Juice of 1 lime	
	Salt and black pepper to taste	
1 tbsp	chopped fresh cilantro	15 mL
1/2 cup	sour cream	125 mL
1 tsp	grated lime zest	5 mL
1/4 cup	finely chopped red bell pepper	50 mL

1. Combine sweet potatoes, onion, garlic, stock, cumin, hot pepper flakes and ginger in slow cooker stoneware.

2. Cover and cook on **Low** for 8 to 10 hours or on **High** for 4 to 6 hours, or until sweet potatoes are tender.

3. In a colander, strain soup, reserving liquid. Transfer sweet potato mixture to a blender or food processor. Add 1 cup (250 mL) reserved liquid, peanut butter and lime juice. Process until smooth.

4. Return soup to slow cooker along with remaining liquid. Season to taste with salt and pepper. Stir in cilantro. Cover and cook on **High** for 10 minutes, or until heated through.

5. In a small bowl, combine sour cream and lime zest.

6. Spoon soup into serving bowls. Add a dollop of sour cream mixture and garnish with chopped red pepper.

Springtime Russian Borscht

Makes 6 to 8 servings

No slow cooker cookbook is complete without a good long-cooked borscht. Chock full of vegetables, this glorious ruby-red soup will brighten up even the gloomiest of days.

When beets with tops are not available, substitute additional shredded cabbage or Swiss chard for the beet greens.

Make Ahead
This soup can be assembled up to 24 hours before cooking. Combine ingredients and refrigerate overnight in the slow cooker stoneware. The next day, place stoneware in slow cooker and continue to cook as directed.

• *Slow Cooker Size: 3 1/2 to 6 qt*

4	beets (including tops)	4
I cup	shredded cabbage	250 mL
I cup	finely chopped turnip	250 mL
I	large potato, peeled and finely chopped	I
I	carrot, peeled and shredded or finely chopped	I
I	stalk celery, finely chopped	I
4 cups	vegetable or chicken stock	I L
1/4 cup	ketchup	50 mL
I tsp	paprika	5 mL
1/4 cup	chopped fresh dillweed, divided	50 mL
2 tbsp	red wine vinegar	25 mL
	Salt and black pepper to taste	
1/4 cup	sour cream	50 mL

1. Peel beets and reserve tops. Chop or shred beets.

2. Combine beets, cabbage, turnip, potato, carrot, celery, stock, ketchup, paprika and 2 tbsp (25 mL) dill in slow cooker stoneware.

3. Cover and cook on **Low** for 8 to 10 hours or on **High** for 4 to 6 hours, or until vegetables are tender.

4. Finely chop beet tops. Stir tops and vinegar into slow cooker and season with salt and pepper. Cover and let sit for 5 minutes, or just until beet greens wilt.

5. Spoon soup into individual serving bowls and serve with a dollop of sour cream. Sprinkle soup with remaining dill.

Taco Beef Soup

Serves 4 to 6

This soup can be put together quickly, and it will satisfy a hungry family at the end of the day. Spoon the soup into individual serving bowls and pass toppings such as grated Cheddar, sour cream or crushed tortilla chips.

Make Ahead
This soup can be assembled up to 24 hours before cooking. Complete Step 1 and chill meat mixture completely. Then combine all ingredients in slow cooker stoneware and refrigerate overnight. The next day, place stoneware in slow cooker and continue to cook as directed.

• *Slow Cooker Size: 3 1/2 to 6 qt*

1 1/2 lbs	lean ground beef	750 g
1/2 cup	chopped green onions (about 4)	125 mL
2	cloves garlic, minced	2
1 tsp	ground cumin	5 mL
1 tsp	chili powder	5 mL
1/4 tsp	dried oregano leaves	1 mL
2 cups	beef stock	500 mL
1	19-oz (540 mL) can tomatoes, chopped, with juices	1
1	7 1/2-oz (213 mL) can tomato sauce	1
1	4 1/2-oz (127 mL) can chopped mild green chilies, drained	1
1	19-oz (540 mL) can pinto or red kidney beans, rinsed and drained, or 2 cups (500 mL) home-cooked beans (page 145)	1
1/2 tsp	salt	2 mL
1/4 tsp	black pepper	1 mL

1. In a large nonstick skillet over medium-high heat, cook ground beef, green onions and garlic, breaking up meat as it cooks, for 5 to 7 minutes, or until meat is no longer pink.

2. Add cumin, chili powder and oregano. Cook for 1 minute. With a slotted spoon, transfer mixture to slow cooker stoneware.

3. Add stock, tomatoes, tomato sauce, chilies, beans, salt and pepper to slow cooker. Stir to combine.

4. Cover and cook on **Low** for 6 to 10 hours or on **High** for 3 to 4 hours, or until soup is bubbling.

BLT Soup

Makes 6 servings

This fun soup was inspired by my husband's favorite sandwich. It includes all the BLT ingredients, even the shredded lettuce. Serve it with white bread that has been lightly spread with mayonnaise.

For a smoother, creamier consistency, this soup can be pureed. After the soup has cooked, transfer to a blender or food processor and, in batches, puree until smooth. Return to slow cooker and season to taste with salt and pepper.

Make Ahead

This soup can be assembled up to 24 hours before cooking. Prepare ingredients as directed, assemble in slow cooker stoneware and refrigerate overnight. The next day, place stoneware in slow cooker and continue to cook as directed.

• *Slow Cooker Size: 3 ½ to 6 qt*

½ lb	bacon, finely chopped (6 to 8 slices)	250 g
1	large onion, finely chopped	1
2	cloves garlic, minced	2
1	19-oz (540 mL) can Italian-style (page 103) stewed tomatoes, including juices	1
4 cups	chicken stock	1 L
1 tsp	dried basil leaves	5 mL
1 tbsp	tomato paste	15 mL
½ tsp	granulated sugar	2 mL
	Salt and black pepper to taste	
1 cup	finely shredded lettuce	250 mL

1. In a large nonstick skillet on medium-high heat, cook bacon, onion and garlic, stirring occasionally, for 5 minutes, or until onion is translucent. With a slotted spoon, transfer mixture to slow cooker stoneware.

2. Add tomatoes, stock, basil, tomato paste and sugar to slow cooker.

3. Cover and cook on **Low** for 6 to 10 hours or on **High** for 3 to 4 hours, or until soup is bubbling. Season with salt and pepper.

4. Spoon into individual serving bowls and sprinkle with shredded lettuce.

Tomato Paste

Tomato paste is made from tomatoes that have been cooked for several hours until the sauce has thickened and has a rich, concentrated flavor and color. Look for tomato paste in squeezable tubes rather than cans. It is especially easy to use when a recipe calls for smaller quantities. The tubes can be found in Italian grocery stores and some supermarkets. Refrigerate after opening.

Tuscan Pepper and Bean Soup

Makes 4 to 6 servings

This tasty vegetarian soup is filling and flavorful, and it is even better reheated the next day. Serve it with bruschetta and fresh fruit.

• *Slow Cooker Size: 3 1/2 to 6 qt*

1	leek, white and light-green part only, well rinsed and sliced	1
1	potato, peeled and diced	1
2	cloves garlic, minced	2
4	roasted red peppers (page 161), finely chopped	4
4 cups	vegetable or chicken stock	1 L
1/4 tsp	dried thyme leaves	1 mL
1/4 tsp	dried rosemary leaves	1 mL
1/2 tsp	salt	2 mL
1/4 tsp	black pepper	1 mL
1	19-oz (540 mL) can white kidney beans, rinsed and drained, or 2 cups (500 mL) home-cooked beans (page 145)	1
1 cup	cooked bow tie, rotini or other small pasta (optional)	250 mL

1. Combine leek, potato, garlic, red peppers, stock, thyme, rosemary, salt, pepper and beans in slow cooker stoneware. Stir to combine.

2. Cover and cook on **Low** for 6 to 10 hours or on **High** for 3 to 4 hours, or until hot and bubbling.

3. Add cooked pasta if using. Cover and cook on **High** for 15 to 20 minutes, or until heated through.

Bruschetta

In a bowl, combine 4 finely chopped tomatoes, 2 minced cloves garlic, 1/4 cup (50 mL) chopped fresh basil, 2 tbsp (25 mL) olive oil, 1/2 tsp (2 mL) salt and 1/4 tsp (1 mL) black pepper. Spoon mixture onto 12 toasted or grilled baguette slices and sprinkle with 1/4 cup (50 mL) grated Parmesan cheese. Broil or grill for 1 minute, or until cheese melts. Makes 12.

Poultry

Apple Chicken

Makes 4 to 6 servings

This is a wonderful dish to serve when the weather turns cooler and the nights are longer. Use apples that keep their shape and texture during cooking, such as Ida Red, Mutsu (Crispin) and Northern Spy.

• *Slow Cooker Size: 3 1/2 to 6 qt*

12	skinless chicken drumsticks or thighs	12
1 tsp	dried thyme leaves	5 mL
1/2 tsp	salt	2 mL
1/2 tsp	black pepper	2 mL
2	apples, unpeeled, thickly sliced	2
1	onion, sliced	1
1/2 cup	apple cider or apple juice	125 mL
1 1/2 tsp	cider vinegar	7 mL
1 tbsp	cornstarch	15 mL

1. Place chicken in slow cooker stoneware. Sprinkle with thyme, salt and pepper.

2. Add apples and onion. Pour apple cider over chicken.

3. Cover and cook on **Low** for 5 to 7 hours or on **High** for 2 1/2 to 4 hours, or until chicken is no longer pink inside. Transfer chicken to a serving plate and keep warm.

4. In a small bowl or jar (page 177), combine vinegar and cornstarch. Whisk into slow cooker. Cover and cook on **High** for 15 to 20 minutes, or until thickened. Spoon over chicken.

Caramelized Onion Chicken

Makes 4 to 6 servings

In this dish, a sweet, tangy sauce forms as the chicken cooks. Serve with boiled or baked potatoes or, for a change, try serving with potato dumplings, German spätzle or Italian gnocchi. You'll find them in the fresh pasta/deli aisle or frozen food section of the supermarket. Toss the cooked dumplings with melted butter and add a sprinkle of chopped fresh parsley or dill for a touch of color and flavor.

• Slow Cooker Size: 3 1/2 to 6 qt

12	skinless chicken thighs or drumsticks	12
1/2 tsp	salt	2 mL
1/4 tsp	black pepper	1 mL
1 tbsp	butter	15 mL
1	sweet onion, sliced	1
1/2 cup	raspberry jam, preferably seedless	125 mL
1 tbsp	red wine vinegar	15 mL
1 tbsp	soy sauce	15 mL
2 tsp	grated gingerroot, or 1 tsp (5 mL) ground ginger	10 mL
1/2 tsp	dried rosemary leaves, crumbled	2 mL

1. Place chicken thighs in slow cooker stoneware and sprinkle with salt and pepper.

2. In a medium skillet, melt butter on medium-high heat. Add onion and cook, stirring, for 2 minutes. Reduce heat to medium and cook for 10 to 12 minutes longer, stirring often, until onions are tender and golden brown. Spread over top of chicken.

3. In a bowl, combine jam, vinegar, soy sauce, gingerroot and rosemary. Pour over chicken and onions.

4. Cover and cook on **Low** for 5 to 7 hours or on **High** for 2 1/2 to 4 hours, or until chicken is no longer pink inside.

Brunswick Stew

Makes 6 servings

Dating back to 1828 in Brunswick County, Virginia, this stew was originally made with squirrel and onion, but today chicken is a more popular choice! Serve with coleslaw and warm baking powder biscuits slathered with butter.

• *Slow Cooker Size: 3 1/2 to 6 qt*

3	slices bacon	3
2 tbsp	all-purpose flour	25 mL
I tsp	salt	5 mL
1/2 tsp	black pepper	2 mL
1/2 tsp	dried marjoram leaves	2 mL
1/2 tsp	hot red pepper flakes	2 mL
2 lbs	boneless skinless chicken thighs, cut in I-inch (2.5 cm) pieces	I kg
2 cups	chicken stock, divided	500 mL
2 cups	diced peeled potatoes	500 mL
3	carrots, peeled and cut in I-inch (2.5 cm) slices	3
2	stalks celery, chopped	2
I	19-oz (540 mL) can tomatoes, chopped, with juices	I
2	cloves garlic, minced	2
1/2 cup	ketchup	125 mL
2 tbsp	packed brown sugar	25 mL
I tbsp	Worcestershire sauce	15 mL
I tsp	dry mustard	5 mL
1/2 tsp	ground ginger	2 mL
2 cups	frozen and defrosted lima beans	500 mL
I cup	fresh or frozen and defrosted corn kernels	250 mL

1. In a large skillet on medium-high heat, cook bacon for 5 to 7 minutes, or until crisp. Transfer to a paper-towel lined plate, reserving drippings.

2. In a heavy plastic bag, combine flour, salt, pepper, marjoram and hot pepper flakes. In batches, add chicken to flour mixture and toss to coat.

3. In skillet with reserved drippings, cook chicken in batches on medium-high heat, stirring occasionally, until browned on all sides. With a slotted spoon, transfer to slow cooker stoneware.

4. Add 1 cup (250 mL) stock to skillet and bring to a boil, stirring to scrape up any browned bits. Transfer stock mixture to slow cooker. Add reserved bacon, remaining stock, potatoes, carrots, celery, tomatoes, garlic, ketchup, brown sugar, Worcestershire, mustard and ginger.

5. Cover and cook on **Low** for 6 to 8 hours or on **High** for 3 to 5 hours, or until vegetables are tender and stew is bubbling.

6. Add lima beans and corn. Cover and cook on **High** for 15 to 20 minutes, or until beans and corn are heated through.

Quick and Easy Creamy Coleslaw

In a bowl, combine 3 cups (750 mL) finely shredded cabbage, 2 grated carrots and 2 chopped green onions.

In a small bowl or measuring cup, combine $\frac{1}{4}$ cup (50 mL) mayonnaise, $\frac{1}{4}$ cup (50 mL) plain yogurt or sour cream, 1 tbsp (15 mL) white vinegar, 1 tsp (5 mL) granulated sugar, $\frac{1}{2}$ tsp (2 mL) celery seed, $\frac{1}{2}$ tsp (2 mL) prepared mustard and $\frac{1}{4}$ tsp (1 mL) black pepper. Pour over cabbage mixture and toss well. Cover and refrigerate for up to 24 hours. Makes 4 to 6 servings.

Chicken Cacciatore

This Italian specialty
is prepared hunter
style, which means
it is slowly cooked in a
tomato sauce seasoned
with onions and herbs.

I like to serve this
over plain spaghetti
or noodles, but you
can also serve it with
roasted potatoes
(page 121) and a
green salad.

• *Slow Cooker Size: 3 1/2 to 6 qt*

1/4 cup	all-purpose flour	50 mL
1/2 tsp	salt	2 mL
1 tsp	dried Italian herb seasoning (page 36)	5 mL
1/4 tsp	black pepper	1 mL
3 lbs	boneless skinless chicken thighs	1.5 kg
1	onion, chopped	1
8 oz	mushrooms, sliced (about 3 cups/750 mL)	250 g
2	stalks celery, chopped	2
2	cloves garlic, minced	2
1	14-oz (398 mL) can tomatoes, chopped, with juices	1
1 cup	pasta sauce or tomato sauce	250 mL
2 tbsp	dry white wine	25 mL
1	bay leaf	1
1/4 cup	chopped fresh parsley	50 mL
2 tbsp	grated Parmesan cheese	25 mL

1. In a large heavy-duty plastic bag, combine flour, salt, Italian seasoning and pepper. In batches, toss chicken pieces in flour mixture to coat. Place chicken in slow cooker stoneware.

2. Add onion, mushrooms, celery, garlic, tomatoes, pasta sauce, wine, bay leaf and parsley to slow cooker.

3. Cover and cook on **Low** for 5 to 7 hours or on **High** for 2 1/2 to 4 hours, or until chicken is tender and no longer pink inside. Discard bay leaf. Serve sprinkled with Parmesan cheese.

Clubhouse Chicken

Makes 4 servings

Thanks go to my neighbor Caroline Wolff for passing along her favorite family slow cooker recipe. Everyone loves a clubhouse sandwich, so this combination will please kids and parents alike.

A can of condensed soup is used because it holds up well through the long slow-cooking process. Choose a reduced-sodium soup if possible.

• *Slow Cooker Size: 3 1/2 to 6 qt*

8	boneless skinless chicken thighs	8
1 tbsp	Dijon mustard	15 ml
4	thin slices Black Forest ham, halved	4
8	slices Swiss cheese	8
1 tsp	dried thyme leaves	5 mL
1/2 tsp	paprika	2 mL
1	10-oz (284 mL) can condensed cream of mushroom soup, undiluted	1
1/2 cup	evaporated milk	125 mL
4	slices bacon, cooked and crumbled	4

1. Lay chicken thighs, smooth side down, between two pieces of waxed paper and pound with a mallet until 1/4 inch (5 mm) thick. Spread inside of each thigh with mustard. Place a piece of ham on each thigh. Place a slice of cheese on top of ham. Roll up chicken and secure with a toothpick.

2. Lay chicken rolls in slow cooker stoneware. Sprinkle with thyme and paprika.

3. In a bowl, whisk together soup and milk and pour over chicken.

4. Cover and cook on **Low** for 5 to 6 hours, or until chicken is no longer pink inside.

5. Using a slotted spoon, transfer chicken to a plate and discard toothpicks. Whisk sauce in slow cooker until blended and spoon sauce over each serving. Sprinkle with crumbled bacon.

Coconut Curry Chicken

Makes 6 servings

This spicy, fragrant stew is traditionally served over steamed rice (page 73).

• *Slow Cooker Size: 3 1/2 to 6 qt*

1/2 cup	all-purpose flour	125 mL
1/2 tsp	salt	2 mL
1/2 tsp	black pepper	2 mL
12	skinless chicken thighs	12
1 tbsp	vegetable oil	15 mL
2	onions, chopped	2
4	cloves garlic, minced	4
1 tbsp	curry powder, or 2 tbsp (25 mL) mild curry paste	15 mL
1/2 cup	chicken stock	125 mL
1	14-oz (400 mL) can coconut milk	1
4	carrots, peeled and sliced	4
1	19-oz (540 mL) can chickpeas, rinsed and drained, or 2 cups (500 mL) home-cooked chickpeas (page 145)	1
1 cup	fresh or frozen and defrosted green peas or snow peas	250 mL L
1	Granny Smith apple, unpeeled and cut in 1-inch (2.5 cm) chunks	1
1 cup	plain yogurt	250 mL
1/2 cup	cashew nuts	125 mL
1/4 cup	shredded coconut, toasted	50 mL

1. In a shallow dish, combine flour, salt and pepper. Add chicken thighs to flour mixture and toss to coat. Place chicken in bottom of slow cooker stoneware, reserving excess flour.

2. In a large nonstick skillet, heat oil over medium-high heat. Add onions, garlic and curry powder. Cook, stirring, for 3 minutes, or until onions are translucent and fragrant. Sprinkle with reserved seasoned flour and cook, stirring, for 1 minute.

3. Stir in stock and coconut milk and bring to a boil. Add carrots and chickpeas. Mix well and pour over chicken in slow cooker.

4. Cover and cook on **Low** for 5 to 7 hours or on **High** for $2\frac{1}{2}$ to 4 hours, or until chicken is no longer pink inside, vegetables are tender and curry is bubbling.

5. Stir in green peas, apple and yogurt.

6. Cover and cook on **High** for 15 to 20 minutes, or until warmed through. Serve garnished with cashews and coconut.

Toasting Coconut

Spread flaked or shredded coconut on a baking sheet. Toast at 300°F (150°C) for 10 to 12 minutes, or until golden.

Jamaican Jerk Chicken Sandwiches

Makes 4 to 6 servings

There is nothing more Jamaican in flavor than jerk seasoning. The ingredients vary depending on the cook, but it is primarily a combination of hot chilies, thyme, cinnamon, ginger, allspice, ground cloves, fresh garlic and onions. Jerk seasoning is sold in dried or paste form, or as a liquid marinade. If you are using the marinade, use $1/4$ cup (50 mL) and reduce the chicken stock to $1/4$ cup (50 mL).

These sandwiches are great for casual get-togethers. Let guests serve themselves, and round out the menu with a basket of tortilla chips and a tray of raw veggies and dip.

• *Slow Cooker Size: 3$1/2$ to 6 qt*

2 tbsp	Caribbean jerk seasoning powder or paste	25 mL
2 lbs	boneless skinless chicken thighs	1 kg
1	red bell pepper, seeded and chopped	1
1	onion, finely chopped	1
$1/2$ cup	chicken stock	125 mL
$1/4$ cup	ketchup	50 mL
1	green bell pepper, seeded and chopped	1
2 tbsp	dark rum (optional)	25 mL
6	kaiser rolls, split	6

1. Rub jerk seasoning generously over chicken thighs.

2. Place red pepper and onion in bottom of slow cooker stoneware. Place seasoned thighs over vegetables.

3. In a small bowl, combine stock and ketchup. Pour over chicken.

4. Cover and cook on **Low** for 5 to 7 hours or on **High** for 2$1/2$ to 4 hours, or until chicken is no longer pink inside.

5. Transfer chicken to a bowl and shred by pulling meat apart with two forks. Skim fat from sauce in slow cooker.

6. Return chicken to slow cooker with green pepper and rum, if using, and mix well with sauce. Cover and cook on **High** for 15 to 20 minutes, or until pepper has softened slightly. With a slotted spoon, spoon chicken and vegetable mixture into kaiser rolls.

Turmeric

Turmeric is the ground root of a tropical plant. It has an intense golden yellow color and gingery flavor. If you wish, you can substitute ground ginger. The color won't be as intense, but the flavor will still be good.

Moroccan Chicken Stew

Makes 4 to 6 servings

For a simple but satisfying Moroccan-style dinner, serve this stew with warm pita bread, hummus and orange wedges. Or serve the chicken over couscous, which only takes minutes to prepare and will soak up all the delicious sauce. (Prepare the couscous according to package directions.)

- Slow Cooker Size: 3 1/2 to 6 qt

8 to 12	skinless chicken drumsticks	8 to 12
1	19-oz (540 mL) can chickpeas, rinsed and drained, or 2 cups (500 mL) home-cooked chickpeas (page 145)	1
1/2 cup	diced tomato	125 mL
1 cup	baby carrots	250 mL
1	14-oz (398 mL) can pineapple tidbits or chunks, with juices	1
1	large onion, chopped	1
2	cloves garlic, minced	2
2 tbsp	lemon juice	25 mL
1 tsp	salt	5 mL
1 tsp	dried marjoram leaves	5 mL
1 tsp	paprika	5 mL
1/2 tsp	ground cumin	2 mL
1/4 tsp	ground turmeric	1 mL
Pinch	ground cinnamon	Pinch
1 cup	diced green beans	250 mL
1/4 cup	pimento-stuffed green olives	50 mL
1/4 cup	chopped fresh mint or cilantro	50 mL

1. Place chicken in slow cooker stoneware. Add chickpeas, tomato and carrots.

2. In a bowl, combine pineapple and juices, onion, garlic, lemon juice, salt, marjoram, paprika, cumin, turmeric and cinnamon. Pour over meat and vegetables.

3. Cover and cook on **Low** for 5 to 7 hours or on **High** for 2 1/2 to 4 hours, or until chicken is no longer pink inside.

4. Add green beans. Cover and cook on **High** for 20 to 25 minutes, or until beans are tender.

5. Stir in olives and mint.

PBJ Chicken Stew

Makes 4 to 6 servings

Peanut butter, jelly and chicken stew? You bet, and it's delicious! The jelly adds a touch of sweetness and the peanut butter lends a nutty flavor. Of course, you must serve it with slices of white bread to soak up the extra sauce. Accompany with a garden salad and apple pie with ice cream for dessert.

• *Slow Cooker Size: 3 1/2 to 6 qt*

8	skinless chicken breasts, thighs or drumsticks	8
I	large onion, chopped	I
8 oz	mushrooms, quartered	250 g
2 tbsp	chopped fresh parsley	25 mL
I cup	chicken stock	250 mL
1/2 cup	chunky peanut butter	125 mL
1/4 cup	grape jelly or berry jam or jelly	50 mL
I tbsp	tomato paste	15 mL
1/2 tsp	salt	2 mL
I	red bell pepper, seeded and cut in 1/2-inch (1 cm) strips	I
2 tbsp	chopped peanuts	25 mL

1. Place chicken pieces in slow cooker stoneware. Sprinkle onion, mushrooms and parsley around and on top of chicken.

2. In a bowl, combine stock, peanut butter, jelly, tomato paste and salt. Pour sauce over chicken and vegetables.

3. Cover and cook on **Low** for 5 to 7 hours or on **High** for 2 1/2 to 4 hours, or until chicken is no longer pink inside.

4. Add red pepper. Cover and cook on **High** for 20 to 25 minutes, or until pepper is tender.

5. Serve garnished with chopped peanuts.

Coconut Curry Chicken (page 60)
Overleaf: Turkish Winglets (page 27)

Polenta Tamale Pie

**Makes 6 to
8 servings**

Ground chicken, salsa
and pre-packaged
polenta are combined in
this easy, snappy dish
with a Mexican flare.

Salsa is Spanish for
sauce. Mexican cuisine
includes many raw and
cooked salsas based on
tomatoes or tomatillos
with chilies. Salsa can
be chunky or smooth,
and it can be spicy,
medium or mild. Use
your family's favorite.

Make Ahead
This dish can be
completely assembled
up to 24 hours before
cooking. Refrigerate
overnight in the slow
cooker stoneware.
The next day, place
stoneware in slow
cooker and continue
to cook as directed.

• *Slow Cooker Size: 5 to 6 qt*

1 tbsp	vegetable oil	15 mL
1 lb	lean ground chicken or turkey	500 g
1 tbsp	chili powder	15 mL
1 tsp	ground cumin	5 mL
1 ½ cups	salsa	375 mL
1	14-oz (398 mL) can refried beans	1
2 tbsp	chopped fresh cilantro	25 mL
1	1-lb (500 g) roll prepared polenta, sliced in 20 rounds	1
3 cups	grated Cheddar cheese, divided	750 mL

1. In a large nonstick skillet, heat oil on medium-high heat. Add ground chicken and cook, breaking up meat with a spoon, for about 5 minutes, or until chicken is no longer pink.

2. Add chili powder and cumin, and cook, stirring, for 1 minute.

3. Add salsa and refried beans. Simmer until mixture thickens, about 5 minutes. Stir in cilantro.

4. Place half the polenta slices in bottom of lightly greased slow cooker stoneware. Spoon chicken mixture over polenta. Top with 1½ cups (375 mL) cheese and remaining polenta.

5. Cover and cook on **Low** for 4 to 6 hours, or until heated through and bubbling. Sprinkle with remaining cheese. Cover and cook on **Low** for 10 minutes, or until cheese melts.

> ### Polenta
>
> Polenta is a mush made from cornmeal. It is available ready-to-eat and packaged in a plastic wrapper in the refrigerated section or deli department of the supermarket.

Bistro Beef and Beer Stew
(page 86)

Chicken with Orange Gremolata

This is a chicken version of an Italian dish that is traditionally made with veal shanks. Pass any extra gremolata — a flavorful mix of parsley, garlic and orange zest (be sure to grate the zest before juicing the orange).

For an authentic Italian meal, serve this with risotto and a good Italian red wine.

• *Slow Cooker Size: 5 to 6 qt*

1	roasting chicken (3 to 6 lbs/1.5 to 3 kg)	1
1 tbsp	vegetable oil	15 mL
1	onion, finely chopped	1
1	stalk celery, finely chopped	1
2	cloves garlic, minced	2
2	carrots, peeled and sliced	2
1	red bell pepper, seeded and coarsely chopped	1
1 tsp	dried rosemary leaves, crumbled	5 mL
½ tsp	dried thyme leaves	2 mL
1	19-oz (540 mL) can stewed tomatoes, with juices	1
	Juice of 1 orange	
2 tbsp	dry white wine or chicken stock	25 mL

GREMOLATA

⅓ cup	chopped fresh parsley	75 mL
1 tsp	grated orange zest	5 mL
1	clove garlic, minced	1

1. Rinse chicken inside and out and pat dry. Trim off excess fat. Truss chicken loosely.

2. In a large nonstick skillet, heat oil on medium-high heat. Brown chicken on all sides, beginning with breast side down (this should take about 20 minutes in total). Use two wooden spoons to turn bird so you don't puncture skin.

3. Place chicken in slow cooker stoneware breast side up.

4. Drain off all but 1 tbsp (15 mL) fat from skillet and reduce heat to medium. Add onion, celery, garlic, carrots, red pepper, rosemary and thyme. Cook, stirring, for about 5 minutes, or until vegetables are soft.

5. Add tomatoes with juices, orange juice and wine to skillet. Bring to a boil, reduce heat and simmer for 5 minutes, or until thickened. Pour over chicken.

6. Cover and cook on **Low** for 7 to 9 hours or on **High** for $3\frac{1}{2}$ to 4 hours, or until a meat thermometer inserted in thigh reads 170°F (77°C). (Removing lid of slow cooker releases heat, which will lengthen the cooking time. Do not remove lid until minimum cooking time.)

7. Transfer chicken to a plate and cover loosely with foil. Let sit for 10 minutes before carving. Skim fat from sauce.

8. Meanwhile, to prepare gremolata, in a bowl, combine parsley, orange zest and garlic.

9. Serve chicken with vegetable sauce and sprinkle gremolata over each serving.

Baked Chicken with Mustard Barbecue Sauce

Makes 6 servings

A century ago, spicy English mustards were too pungent for the North American palate. In the early 1900s, bright-yellow prepared mustard was invented and we now slather it on everything from sandwiches to pretzels. It also adds a tangy zip to this barbecue sauce. Serve the chicken with creamy coleslaw (page 57) and steamed corn.

- Slow Cooker Size: 3 1/2 to 6 qt

12	skinless chicken drumsticks	12
1	19-oz (540 mL) can tomatoes, drained	1
1/4 cup	packed brown sugar	50 mL
3 tbsp	cider vinegar	45 mL
2 tbsp	prepared mustard	25 mL
1 1/2 tsp	Worcestershire sauce	7 mL
1 tsp	salt	5 mL
1/2 tsp	black pepper	2 mL

1. Place chicken in slow cooker stoneware.

2. In a blender or food processor, puree tomatoes, brown sugar, vinegar, mustard, Worcestershire, salt and pepper until smooth. Pour sauce over chicken.

3. Cover and cook on **Low** for 5 to 7 hours or on **High** for 2 1/2 to 4 hours, or until chicken is no longer pink inside. For a thicker sauce, transfer chicken to a serving platter and keep warm. Transfer sauce to a saucepan and bring to a boil. Boil gently until reduced by half or sauce reaches desired consistency. Pour sauce over chicken.

Pesto

Pesto can be purchased fresh or bottled in the supermarket, but you can also make your own.

In a food processor, finely chop 2 cups (500 mL) packed fresh basil leaves, 3 cloves garlic, 1/2 cup (125 mL) grated Parmesan cheese, 1/4 cup (50 mL) pine nuts, 1/4 tsp (1 mL) salt and 1/4 tsp (1 mL) black pepper. With the food processor running, add 1/3 cup (75 mL) olive oil in a thin, steady stream. This pesto can be refrigerated for up to three days or frozen for up to six months. Makes about 1 cup (250 mL).

Cheesy Pesto Pasta

**Makes 8 to
10 servings**

Round out this
deliciously fragrant
Italian dish with toasted
garlic bread (page 129)
and a green salad. For
a wonderful splash of
color, use rainbow-
colored pasta.

You can also use ½ cup
(125 mL) crumbled goat
cheese in place of the
last 1½ cups (375 mL)
grated mozzarella.

• *Slow Cooker Size: 3½ to 6 qt*

4 cups	dried fusilli, penne or other small pasta	1 L
1 tbsp	vegetable oil	15 mL
1 lb	lean ground chicken or turkey	500 g
1	onion, chopped	1
1	19-oz (540 mL) can Italian-style (page 103) stewed tomatoes, with juices	1
½ cup	basil pesto	125 mL
¼ cup	chopped fresh parsley	50 mL
½ tsp	salt	2 mL
¼ tsp	black pepper	1 mL
¼ cup	grated Parmesan cheese	50 mL
3 cups	grated mozzarella or pre-shredded three-cheese blend, divided	750 mL

1. In a large pot of boiling salted water, cook pasta for 7 to 10 minutes, or until almost tender but still firm. Drain and return to pot.

2. Meanwhile, in a large nonstick skillet, heat oil over medium-high heat. Add chicken and cook, breaking up meat with the back of a spoon, for about 5 minutes, or until browned.

3. Drain any accumulated fat from skillet and stir in onion. Cook, stirring frequently, until softened, about 4 minutes.

4. Add tomatoes, pesto, parsley, salt and pepper. Simmer for 5 minutes.

5. Stir sauce into pasta with Parmesan and half the grated cheese. Mix well and transfer to lightly greased slow cooker stoneware.

6. Cover and cook on **Low** for 4 to 6 hours or on **High** for 2 to 3 hours, or until hot and bubbly.

7. Sprinkle with remaining cheese. Cover and cook on **High** for 15 to 20 minutes, or until cheese has melted.

Four Cs Enchiladas

Makes 4 to 6 servings

The four Cs — chicken, chilies, corn and cheese — are the basis for this Mexican specialty consisting of tortillas rolled around a filling and topped with tomato sauce and cheese. Usually cooked shredded meat is used, but I have substituted ground chicken.

Tight for time? Look for pre-shredded Mexican blend cheese.

• Slow Cooker Size: 5 to 6 qt

1 tbsp	vegetable oil	15 mL
1 lb	lean ground chicken	500 g
2 tsp	ground cumin	10 mL
2 tsp	garlic powder	10 mL
1/2 tsp	dried oregano leaves	2 mL
1/4 tsp	hot red pepper flakes	1 mL
1	4 1/2-oz (127 mL) can chopped mild green chilies, including liquid	1
1 cup	fresh or frozen and defrosted corn kernels	250 mL
1	onion, finely chopped	1
1	19-oz (540 mL) can tomatoes, drained and chopped, juices reserved	1
8	10-inch (25 cm) flour tortillas	8
2 cups	grated Cheddar or Monterey Jack cheese, divided	500 mL
1 1/2 cups	salsa	375 mL

1. In a large nonstick skillet, heat oil over medium-high heat. Add chicken and cook, breaking up meat with a spoon, until browned, about 7 to 8 minutes.

2. Add cumin, garlic powder, oregano and hot pepper flakes. Cook, stirring, for 1 to 2 minutes, or until fragrant.

3. Stir in chilies, corn, onion and drained tomatoes. Bring mixture to a boil, reduce heat and simmer for 5 minutes, or until slightly thickened.

4. Pour reserved tomato juices into a large bowl. Dip each tortilla in juices to coat lightly. Spoon chicken mixture over tortillas. Sprinkle each tortilla with about 2 tbsp (25 mL) cheese.

5. Fold tortilla over filling and place in lightly greased slow cooker stoneware, seam side down, in layers if necessary. Top each layer with salsa.

6. Cover and cook on **Low** for 4 to 5 hours, or until hot and bubbling.

7. Sprinkle remaining cheese over salsa. Cover and cook on **High** for 15 to 20 minutes, or until cheese melts.

Vegetable-stuffed Chicken with Mushroom Sauce

Makes 4 servings

Using inexpensive chicken thighs makes this dish an economical family meal. But don't let the recipe fool you — it's perfect for entertaining as well. Serve over cooked noodles or steamed rice (page 73).

The French term julienne refers to food cut in matchstick-sized pieces. To julienne carrots, first cut in half widthwise, then cut into thin strips.

Purchase chicken thighs in economical family packs. Divide into meal-sized portions, wrap in plastic wrap and freeze in freezer bags.

• *Slow Cooker Size: 3 1/2 to 6 qt*

8	boneless skinless chicken thighs	8
I tsp	salt	5 mL
1/2 tsp	black pepper	2 mL
I	small carrot, peeled and cut in julienne strips	I
1/2	red bell pepper, seeded and cut in 16 strips	1/2
2	green onions, cut in thin strips	2
2 cups	sliced mushrooms	500 mL
I	onion, finely chopped	I
1/2 tsp	dried thyme leaves	2 mL
1/2 tsp	dried sage leaves	2 mL
3 tbsp	all-purpose flour	45 mL
I	13-oz (385 mL) can evaporated milk	I
I tbsp	chopped fresh parsley	15 mL

1. Place chicken thighs smooth side down on work surface. Sprinkle with salt and pepper. Lay 2 or 3 carrot strips, 2 pepper strips and a few green onion strips along one end of thigh. Roll up and secure each with a toothpick.

2. Lay chicken bundles in bottom of slow cooker stoneware. Sprinkle mushrooms, onion, thyme and sage on top of chicken.

3. In a small saucepan, whisk flour into milk. Cook on medium heat, stirring constantly, for 5 to 7 minutes, or until thickened. Pour over chicken and vegetables in slow cooker.

4. Cover and cook on **Low** for 6 to 8 hours, or until chicken is no longer pink inside. With a slotted spoon, transfer chicken bundles to serving plate. Whisk sauce in slow cooker until smooth and pour over chicken. Sprinkle with chopped parsley.

Creamy White Chicken Chili

Makes 6 to 8 servings

This creamy, stew-like chili is different from the typical red tomato-based versions. Nevertheless, the flavors are bold, making it a delicious alternative. Serve it with steamed rice (page 73) or bread.

To save time, you can use lean ground chicken in place of the chicken thighs. Reduce the oil to 1 tbsp (15 mL), brown the meat in the oil with the spices, then add to the slow cooker along with the stock, beans and chilies. You will not have to shred the meat.

• *Slow Cooker Size: 3 1/2 to 6 qt*

3 tbsp	vegetable oil, divided	45 mL
2 lbs	boneless skinless chicken thighs	1 kg
1	onion, finely chopped	1
2	cloves garlic, minced	2
1 tsp	ground cumin	5 mL
1 tsp	dried oregano leaves	5 mL
1/2 tsp	black pepper	2 mL
1/4 tsp	cayenne pepper	1 mL
1	10-oz (284 mL) can condensed chicken broth, undiluted	1
2	19-oz (540 mL) cans white kidney beans, rinsed and drained, or 4 cups (1 L) home-cooked beans (page 145)	2
2	4 1/2-oz (127 mL) cans chopped mild green chilies, including liquid	2
1 tsp	salt	5 mL
1 cup	sour cream	250 mL
1/2 cup	whipping (35%) cream	125 mL
1 cup	grated Monterey Jack cheese	250 mL

1. In a large nonstick skillet, heat 2 tbsp (25 mL) oil over medium-high heat. Add chicken and cook for 5 to 7 minutes per side, or until browned. Place chicken in slow cooker stoneware.

2. Add remaining oil to skillet and heat. Add onion, garlic, cumin, oregano, black pepper and cayenne. Cook, stirring, for 3 minutes, or until onion is softened. Transfer to slow cooker.

3. Pour chicken broth into skillet and bring to a boil, scraping up any browned bits. Pour over chicken and seasonings in slow cooker.

4. Cover and cook on **Low** for 5 to 7 hours or on **High** for 3 to 4 hours, or until hot and bubbling, and chicken is no longer pink inside.

5. Remove chicken from slow cooker and shred with a fork. Return shredded chicken to slow cooker. Stir in beans, chilies, salt, sour cream and whipping cream.

6. Cover and cook on **High** for 15 to 20 minutes, or until heated through.

7. Spoon into serving bowls and sprinkle with grated cheese.

Steamed Rice

This no-fail method works with many types of rice, including basmati or any white or brown rice.

In a saucepan with a tight-fitting lid, bring $2\frac{1}{2}$ cups (625 mL) water and $\frac{1}{4}$ tsp (1 mL) salt to a boil over medium-high heat. Stir in $1\frac{1}{4}$ cups (300 mL) rice. Cover and reduce heat to low. Simmer white rice for 20 minutes and brown rice for 45 minutes, or until rice is tender and liquid has been absorbed. Fluff with a fork.

Leftover rice will keep in the refrigerator for two days or in the freezer for a month. Makes 4 servings.

Spicy Cuban Turkey Stew

**Makes 4 to
6 servings**

This is a highly distinctive stew with Caribbean flavors. Serve it with rice (page 73) for a delicious and substantial meal.

Buy sweet potatoes with deep orange flesh for this recipe — they are sweeter and moister than the pale yellow sweet potatoes.

• *Slow Cooker Size: 3 1/2 to 6 qt*

1 tbsp	all-purpose flour	15 mL
1/2 tsp	dried thyme leaves	2 mL
1/2 tsp	salt	2 mL
1/4 tsp	ground allspice	1 mL
1/4 tsp	ground ginger	1 mL
1/4 tsp	hot red pepper flakes	1 mL
Pinch	ground nutmeg	Pinch
2	boneless skinless turkey thighs (about 1 1/4 lbs/625 g each), cut in 1-inch (2.5 cm) pieces	2
2 tbsp	vegetable oil	25 mL
1 cup	chicken stock, divided	250 mL
1	sweet potato, peeled and cut in 1-inch (2.5 cm) cubes	1
1	onion, chopped	1
2	19-oz (540 mL) cans black beans, rinsed and drained, or 4 cups (1 L) home-cooked black beans (page 145)	2
1 cup	orange juice	250 mL
2 tsp	lime juice	10 mL
1	red bell pepper, seeded and coarsely chopped	1
1	green bell pepper, seeded and coarsely chopped	1

1. In a heavy plastic bag, combine flour, thyme, salt, allspice, ginger, hot pepper flakes and nutmeg.

2. In batches, add turkey pieces to flour mixture and toss to coat.

3. In a large nonstick skillet, heat 1 tbsp (15 mL) oil on medium-high heat. Cook turkey in batches, adding more oil as needed, for 5 to 7 minutes, or until browned on all sides. With a slotted spoon, transfer turkey to slow cooker.

4. Add ½ cup (125 mL) stock to skillet. Bring to a boil, scraping up any browned bits. Transfer to slow cooker stoneware.

5. Add sweet potato, onion, black beans, orange juice and remaining stock to slow cooker. Stir to combine.

6. Cover and cook on **Low** for 7 to 9 hours or on **High** for 3 to 5 hours, or until vegetables are tender and stew is bubbling.

7. Add lime juice and peppers. Cover and cook on **High** for 15 to 20 minutes, or until peppers are tender.

Cooking Poultry in the Slow Cooker

Cooking times for poultry may be longer in large slow cookers and/or where there is a relatively high proportion of dark meat. For predominantly white-meat dishes, be sure to avoid overcooking. Check after the minimum recommended cooking time.

Spinach and Prosciutto Turkey Rolls

Makes 4 to 6 servings

Wow your guests with these sage-infused turkey rolls. If you have fresh sage growing in your garden, substitute 12 to 15 finely chopped leaves for the dried sage.

Prosciutto is an Italian cured ham with a slightly salty flavor. Make sure the deli slices it paper-thin. A good-quality Black Forest ham can be substituted, if you must.

• *Slow Cooker Size: 6 qt*

1 ½ lbs	turkey breast cutlets (about 6)	750 g
1	10-oz (300 g) package frozen chopped spinach, defrosted and squeezed dry	1
2 tbsp	finely chopped fresh parsley	25 mL
¼ cup	dry bread crumbs	50 mL
3 tbsp	grated Parmesan cheese	45 mL
3 tbsp	chopped toasted almonds (page 151)	45 mL
½ tsp	dried sage leaves, divided	2 mL
½ tsp	black pepper, divided	2 mL
6	thin slices prosciutto or ham	6
¼ tsp	salt	1 mL
¼ tsp	paprika	1 mL
¼ cup	dry white wine	50 mL
¾ cup	chicken stock	175 mL
1 tbsp	all-purpose flour	15 mL
2 tbsp	water	25 mL

1. With a mallet, pound turkey cutlets between two sheets of waxed paper until about ¼ inch (1 cm) thick.

2. In a bowl, combine spinach, parsley, bread crumbs, Parmesan, almonds, ¼ tsp (1 mL) sage and ¼ tsp (1 mL) pepper. Mix well.

3. Place a slice of prosciutto on each cutlet. Spoon about ½ cup (125 mL) spinach mixture on top of prosciutto.

4. Starting at short end, roll up each cutlet, encasing filling. Secure rolls with a toothpick.

5. Place rolls in slow cooker stoneware seam side down and sprinkle with salt, remaining pepper and paprika. Pour wine and stock around rolls.

6. Cover and cook on **Low** for 3 to 5 hours, or until turkey is tender. Remove rolls from slow cooker and keep warm.

7. In a small bowl, whisk together flour, remaining sage and water. Add to slow cooker and whisk in.

8. Cover and cook on **High** for 10 to 15 minutes, or until thickened.

9. Remove toothpicks and cut turkey rolls into $\frac{1}{2}$-inch (1 cm) slices. Spoon sauce over turkey.

Homemade Bread Crumbs

To make your own dry bread crumbs, spread bread slices on a flat surface and let stand overnight, until completely dry and brittle. Break bread into pieces and place in a food processor or blender. Process until bread is in fine crumbs.

Turkey Breast with Bulgur and Feta

Makes 6 servings		

• Slow Cooker Size: 4 to 6 qt

Most major supermarkets stock small turkey breasts on a regular basis. However, you can always find them around long holiday weekends in the summer, Thanksgiving and Christmas. Pop them in the freezer for later use; they will keep for up to six months.

I	single turkey breast, bone in (about 2- to 2½-lbs/1 to 1.25 kg)	I
½ tsp	salt	2 mL
I½ tsp	dried oregano leaves, divided	7 mL
I cup	uncooked bulgur	250 mL
3 tbsp	lemon juice	45 mL
¼ tsp	black pepper	I mL
4	green onions, sliced	4
I	clove garlic, minced	I
I	10-oz (284 mL) can condensed chicken broth, undiluted	I
¼ cup	pitted Kalamata olives (page 29)	50 mL
¼ cup	crumbled feta cheese	50 mL

1. Sprinkle turkey breast with salt and ½ tsp (2 mL) oregano.

2. Combine bulgur, lemon juice, pepper, green onions, garlic, remaining oregano and broth in slow cooker stoneware. Place turkey breast on top of bulgur mixture.

3. Cover and cook on **Low** for 4 to 8 hours, or until a meat thermometer reads 170°F (77°C). Remove turkey from slow cooker and let stand for 5 minutes before slicing.

4. Stir olives and feta into bulgur mixture. Serve with turkey.

Bulgur

A staple in Middle Eastern cooking, bulgur, or cracked wheat, is wheat kernels that have been steamed, dried and crushed. It can be coarse, medium or fine and has a tender, chewy texture.

Turkey Tetrazzini

Makes 4 to 6 servings

This quintessential comfort-food dish is perfect for a family meal. All you need to add is a big green salad. Serve it in shallow soup or pasta bowls and sprinkle a little chopped parsley on top for color and added flavor.

Use your favorite fresh mushrooms in this stew. Try cremini, shiitakes, cèpes or chanterelles.

- *Slow Cooker Size: 3 1/2 to 6 qt*

2 lbs	boneless skinless turkey thighs or breasts, cut in 2- x 1/2-inch (5 x 1 cm) strips	1 kg
1 cup	chicken stock	250 mL
1/2 cup	dry white wine	125 mL
1	onion, finely chopped	1
2 tbsp	chopped fresh parsley	25 mL
1/2 tsp	salt	2 mL
1/4 tsp	dried thyme leaves	1 mL
1/4 tsp	black pepper	1 mL
3 tbsp	cornstarch	45 mL
1/4 cup	water	50 mL
4 oz	fresh mushrooms, sliced	125 g
1/2 cup	table (18%) cream	125 mL
8 oz	dried linguine noodles, broken in 2-inch (5 cm) pieces	250 g
1/2 cup	grated Parmesan cheese, divided	125 mL

1. Combine turkey, stock, wine, onion, parsley, salt, thyme and pepper in slow cooker stoneware.

2. Cover and cook on **Low** for 4 to 5 hours, or until meat is tender and no longer pink inside.

3. In a bowl or jar (page 177), combine cornstarch and water. Stir into slow cooker along with mushrooms. Cover and cook on **High** for 20 minutes.

4. Meanwhile, in a large pot of boiling salted water, cook linguine for 5 to 7 minutes, or until tender. Drain well.

5. Stir cream, noodles and 1/4 cup (50 mL) cheese into slow cooker. Cover and cook on **High** for 5 to 10 minutes, or until heated through.

6. Spoon into serving bowls and top with remaining Parmesan.

Tex-Mex Turkey Pancake

Makes 6 servings

Sure, go ahead and use up the Christmas turkey in sandwiches and soups. Or try something a little different like this rice pancake. It's sure to become a family favorite.

• *Slow Cooker Size: 5 to 6 qt*

2¹/₂ cups	cooked rice (about ³/₄ cup/175 mL uncooked)	625 mL
2	eggs, lightly beaten	2
2 tbsp	butter, melted	25 mL
2 cups	shredded cooked turkey or chicken	500 mL
1	onion, thinly sliced	1
2 cups	salsa	500 mL
¹/₂ cup	sliced black olives	125 mL
1 cup	grated Cheddar or Monterey Jack cheese	250 mL
¹/₄ cup	chopped fresh cilantro	50 mL

1. Cut a 2-foot (60 cm) piece of foil or parchment paper in half lengthwise. Fold each piece in half lengthwise and crisscross strips over bottom and up sides of lightly greased slow cooker stoneware.

2. In a bowl, combine rice, eggs and melted butter. Pour into slow cooker. Sprinkle turkey, onion, salsa and olives over rice mixture. (Mixture will be quite liquid.)

3. Cover and cook on **Low** for 3 to 4 hours, or until hot and bubbly.

4. Sprinkle pancake with cheese and cilantro. Cover and cook on **High** for 10 to 15 minutes, or until cheese is melted. Turn off slow cooker, remove lid and let stand for 5 minutes.

5. Run knife around edge of pancake. Using foil handles, lift pancake out of slow cooker.

Beef and Veal

Anthony's Big Ragu

**Makes 6 to
8 servings**

My good friend
Anthony Scian, a
brilliant computer
engineer, loves to cook.
He will spend Sundays
making a big pot of this
sauce so his family can
enjoy it during the week.
Serve it over hot pasta,
sprinkled with grated
Parmesan cheese.

Anthony's mother taught
him two rules for making
pasta sauce: never use
tomato paste and always
add a little butter and
vinegar at the end for a
smooth, rich flavor.

You can substitute lean
ground turkey for the
pork, or just use 1½ lbs
(750 g) ground beef.

Make Ahead
This dish can be
completely assembled
up to 24 hours before
cooking. Chill ground
meat mixture completely
before combining with
other sauce ingredients.
Refrigerate sauce
overnight in slow cooker
stoneware. The next
day, place stoneware in
slow cooker and continue
to cook as directed.

• *Slow Cooker Size: 3½ to 6 qt*

I lb	lean ground beef	500 g
½ lb	lean ground pork	250 g
2	onions, finely chopped	2
4	cloves garlic, minced	4
I	stalk celery, finely chopped	I
I tbsp	dried Italian herb seasoning (page 36)	15 mL
I	28-oz (796 mL) can tomatoes, chopped, with juices	I
I	carrot, peeled and finely chopped	I
I	red bell pepper, seeded and finely chopped	I
8 oz	mushrooms, sliced	250 g
I	28-oz (796 mL) can pasta sauce	I
3	whole cloves	3
I tbsp	balsamic vinegar	15 mL
2 tbsp	butter (optional)	25 mL

I. In a large nonstick skillet on medium-high heat, combine ground beef, ground pork, onions, garlic, celery and Italian seasoning. Cook, breaking up meat with a spoon, for 8 to 10 minutes, or until vegetables are tender and meat is no longer pink. Drain and transfer to slow cooker stoneware.

2. Add tomatoes, carrot, red pepper, mushrooms, pasta sauce and cloves to slow cooker. Stir to combine.

3. Cover and cook on **Low** for 8 to 10 hours or on **High** for 4 to 6 hours, or until hot and bubbling.

4. Stir in vinegar and butter if using. Cover and cook on **High** for 5 to 10 minutes, or until butter is completely melted.

Beef and Bean Burritos

Looking for a hot and hearty meal to please the whole family? Here's just the recipe. All you need is a crisp salad for a complete dinner.

Make Ahead
This dish can be completely assembled up to 24 hours before cooking. Cook ground beef mixture and cool completely before assembling dish. Refrigerate overnight in the slow cooker stoneware. The next day, place stoneware in slow cooker and continue to cook as directed. You can also cook the entire filling ahead, refrigerate overnight and assemble the burritos the next day. Refrigerate until ready to bake.

• *Slow Cooker Size: 3 1/2 to 6 qt*

2 lbs	lean ground beef	1 kg
1	onion, finely chopped	1
2	cloves garlic, minced	2
1 tbsp	chili powder	15 mL
1 tsp	ground cumin	5 mL
1	14-oz (398 mL) can tomato sauce	1
1 cup	salsa	250 mL
1	19-oz (540 mL) can pinto or Romano beans, rinsed and drained, or 2 cups (500 mL) home-cooked beans (page 145)	1
1 cup	fresh or frozen and defrosted corn kernels	250 mL
10 to 12	10-inch (25 cm) flour tortillas	10 to 12
1 cup	grated Cheddar cheese	250 mL

1. In a large nonstick skillet on medium-high heat, cook ground beef, onion, garlic, chili powder and cumin for 8 to 10 minutes, or until browned, breaking up meat with a spoon. Drain off all fat and transfer meat to slow cooker stoneware.

2. Add tomato sauce, salsa, beans and corn to slow cooker. Stir to combine.

3. Cover and cook on **Low** for 6 to 10 hours or on **High** for 3 to 4 hours, or until hot and bubbling.

4. Divide meat mixture evenly among tortillas and roll up burrito style. Arrange in a 13- x 9-inch (3 L) baking dish. Sprinkle with grated Cheddar.

5. Cover with foil and bake in a preheated 350°F (180°C) oven for 20 minutes, or until burritos are slightly browned.

Classic Homestyle Meatloaf

**Makes 6 to
8 servings**

Everyone loves an
old-fashioned meatloaf.
Serve with mashed
potatoes (pages 93
and 131).

Line the stoneware
with cheesecloth or foil
strips to make it easier
to remove the meatloaf
from the slow cooker.

• *Slow Cooker Size: 3 1/2 to 6 qt*

1	large onion, finely chopped	1
2	stalks celery, finely chopped	2
1	carrot, peeled and shredded	1
1	egg, lightly beaten	1
1 1/2 lbs	lean ground beef	750 g
1 cup	dry bread crumbs	250 mL
1/2 cup	ketchup	125 mL
1 tbsp	garlic powder	15 mL
3/4 tsp	dried thyme leaves	4 mL
3/4 tsp	salt	4 mL
3/4 tsp	black pepper	4 mL

1. In a large bowl, combine onion, celery, carrot, egg,
beef, bread crumbs, ketchup, garlic powder, thyme,
salt and pepper. Using your hands, blend meat
mixture well and press into slow cooker stoneware
lined with foil strips or cheesecloth.

2. Cover and cook on **Low** for 8 to 10 hours or on **High**
for 4 to 6 hours, or until a meat thermometer reads
170°F (77°C). Use foil handles or cheesecloth to
remove meatloaf from slow cooker.

Making Meatloaf in the Slow Cooker

Cut a 2-foot (60 cm) length of foil in half
lengthwise. Fold each strip in half lengthwise,
forming two long strips. Crisscross the strips in
the bottom of the slow cooker, bringing the ends
of the foil strips up and clear of the stoneware
rim. Place the meatloaf directly on the foil strips
and tuck foil ends under lid. When meatloaf is
cooked, remove lid and grasp the ends of the
foil strips to lift out meatloaf.

You can also line the slow cooker with
cheesecloth, using enough material to lift out
the finished meatloaf.

Stuffed Mexican Meatloaf

Makes 4 to 6 servings

This family favorite is like an all-in-one taco dish. Serve with a corn and bean salad over shredded lettuce, with additional salsa on the side.

For an extra kick, substitute Monterey Jack or a nacho cheese blend in place of the Cheddar.

• Slow Cooker Size: 3 1/2 to 6 qt

2 lbs	lean ground beef	1 kg
1	7 1/2-oz (213 mL) can tomato sauce	1
2 tbsp	taco seasoning mix	25 mL
1/3 cup	finely chopped green bell pepper	75 mL
1/3 cup	finely chopped onion	75 mL
2/3 cup	crushed tortilla chips, divided	150 mL
1	egg, lightly beaten	1
2 cups	grated Cheddar cheese, divided	500 mL
1/2 cup	sour cream	125 mL
1	tomato, sliced	1
2 tbsp	chopped fresh cilantro	25 mL

1. In a large bowl, combine ground beef, tomato sauce, taco seasoning mix, green pepper, onion, 1/2 cup (125 mL) tortilla chips and egg. Mix well.

2. In a separate bowl, combine 1 1/2 cups (375 mL) Cheddar and sour cream.

3. Place half the meat mixture in foil- or cheesecloth-lined slow cooker stoneware (page 84), making a well in center of loaf. Spoon sour cream mixture into well. Top with remaining meat mixture.

4. Cover and cook on **Low** for 8 to 10 hours or on **High** for 4 to 6 hours, or until a meat thermometer reads 170°F (77°C).

5. Sprinkle remaining cheese over top of loaf and garnish with remaining crushed tortilla chips, tomato slices and cilantro.

6. Cover and cook on **High** for 5 to 10 minutes, or until cheese is melted.

Bistro Beef and Beer Stew

**Makes 4 to
6 servings**

This is a hearty dish full
of vegetable chunks
and tender beef cubes.
The meat slowly bakes
in a bold sauce of beer,
stock and seasonings
until it is fork-tender.
Serve it with red wine,
a French baguette
and light jazz.

Select lean stewing
beef or trim the excess
fat from the meat before
using. (Trimming may
take a little extra time,
but the result will
be worth it.)

Use your favorite fresh
mushrooms in this stew.
Cremini, shiitakes,
cèpes and chanterelles
can be used in place
of all or some of the
button mushrooms.

- *Slow Cooker Size: 3 1/2 to 6 qt*

1/4 cup	all-purpose flour	50 mL
1 tsp	salt	5 mL
1/2 tsp	dried thyme leaves	2 mL
1/2 tsp	dried marjoram leaves	2 mL
1/2 tsp	black pepper	2 mL
2 lbs	stewing beef, cut in 1-inch (2.5 cm) cubes	1 kg
2 tbsp	vegetable oil	25 mL
1 cup	dark beer, flat (page 45)	250 mL
1 cup	beef stock	250 mL
2 tbsp	tomato paste	25 mL
1 tbsp	Dijon mustard	15 mL
1 tbsp	red wine vinegar	15 mL
2 tsp	Worcestershire sauce	10 mL
1	large onion, chopped	1
4	cloves garlic, minced	4
2 cups	baby carrots	500 mL
8 oz	button mushrooms	250 g
1/2 cup	sour cream	125 mL

1. In a large heavy-duty plastic bag, combine flour, salt, thyme, marjoram and pepper. Add beef to flour mixture in batches and toss to coat.

2. In a large nonstick skillet, heat 1 tbsp (15 mL) oil on medium-high heat. Cook beef in batches, adding more oil as needed, for 8 to 10 minutes, or until browned on all sides. With a slotted spoon, transfer beef to slow cooker stoneware.

3. Add beer and stock to skillet and bring to a boil, stirring to scrape up any brown bits. Transfer to slow cooker.

4. Add tomato paste, mustard, vinegar, Worcestershire, onion, garlic, carrots and mushrooms to slow cooker. Mix well to combine.

5. Cover and cook on **Low** for 8 to 10 hours or **High** for 4 to 6 hours, or until vegetables are tender and stew is bubbling. Stir in sour cream just before serving.

Wine-braised Pot Roast

Makes 6 to 8 servings

Roast beef has to be one of the most popular Sunday dinner entrees. Although traditionally made in the oven, this slow cooker version is delicious. Serve with roasted potatoes (page 121) or mashed potatoes (pages 93 and 131).

Browning helps to enhance the flavor of the meat and eliminate any additional fat, but it is not absolutely necessary in this recipe, if you are pressed for time.

• *Slow Cooker Size: 3 1/2 to 6 qt*

I tbsp	vegetable oil	15 mL
I	3- to 4-lb (1.5 to 2 kg) boneless beef cross rib or rump pot roast	I
4	carrots, peeled and cut in I-inch (2.5 cm) chunks	4
2	stalks celery, sliced	2
6	cloves garlic, peeled	6
I cup	dry red wine	250 mL
I	10-oz (284 mL) can condensed beef consomme, undiluted	I
I tsp	whole black peppercorns	5 mL
2	bay leaves	2
1/2 tsp	dried thyme leaves	2 mL

1. In a large skillet, heat oil on medium-high heat. Add roast and cook, turning with wooden spoons, for 7 to 10 minutes, or until browned on all sides.

2. Transfer meat to slow cooker stoneware. Add carrots, celery, garlic, wine, consomme, peppercorns, bay leaves and thyme to meat.

3. Cover and cook on **Low** for 8 to 12 hours or on **High** for 4 to 6 hours, or until meat is fork-tender.

4. Remove roast from slow cooker and let stand for 15 minutes before carving. Skim fat from juices and discard bay leaves.

5. To serve, slice beef across the grain. Serve with beef juices and vegetables.

Orange Sesame Glazed Pot Roast

**Makes 6 to
8 servings**

This Chinese-inspired roast is a tantalizing blend of sweet and tangy.

Slow cooking helps to tenderize less expensive cuts of meat such as pot roasts, which will benefit from longer cooking on low heat. But if you are short of time, cook on **High** for at least four hours to produce fork-tender meat.

• *Slow Cooker Size: 3 1/2 to 6 qt*

1 tbsp	vegetable oil	15 mL
1	3- to 4-lb (1.5 to 2 kg) boneless beef cross rib, blade roast or brisket	1
1/2 cup	hoisin sauce	125 mL
1	7 1/2-oz (213 mL) can tomato sauce	1
1/4 cup	cider vinegar	50 mL
2 tsp	grated orange zest	10 mL
1/4 cup	orange juice	50 mL
2 tbsp	grated gingerroot, or 1 tsp (5 mL) ground ginger	25 mL
2 tbsp	sesame oil	25 mL

1. In a large skillet, heat vegetable oil on medium-high heat. Add roast, and cook, turning with wooden spoons, for 7 to 10 minutes, or until browned on all sides. Transfer meat to slow cooker stoneware.

2. In a bowl, whisk together hoisin sauce, tomato sauce, vinegar, orange zest, orange juice, gingerroot and sesame oil. Pour over roast.

3. Cover and cook on **Low** for 8 to 12 hours or on **High** for 4 to 6 hours, or until meat is fork-tender.

4. Remove roast from slow cooker and let stand for 15 minutes before carving. Slice beef across the grain and serve with beef juices.

Sesame Oil

Sesame oil is available in pale and dark varieties. Pale sesame oil is usually used for cooking and salad dressings. Dark sesame oil has a much stronger flavor than the pale oil and is usually used as an accent oil, to give a boost of flavor and aroma to a finished dish.

Ginger Beef and Broccoli

Makes 4 to 6 servings

This is just like a stir-fry, only much easier. Serve it with steamed rice (page 73). Stop at your favorite Asian take-out restaurant and pick up an order of egg rolls or pot stickers to accompany this dish. Fortune cookies and green tea complete the meal.

You can substitute 2 cups (500 mL) chopped bok choy or kale for the broccoli.

• Slow Cooker Size: 3 1/2 to 6 qt

I tbsp	vegetable oil	15 mL
I tsp	sesame oil (optional)	5 mL
I lb	outside round or blade beef steak, trimmed and cut in 1/2-inch (1 cm) cubes	500 g
I cup	beef stock	250 mL
1/4 cup	soy sauce	50 mL
I tbsp	dry sherry or lemon juice	15 mL
1/2 tsp	hot Asian chili paste or hot red pepper flakes	2 mL
I	small onion, sliced	I
4	cloves garlic, minced	4
2 tbsp	grated gingerroot	25 mL
I	8-oz (227 mL) can sliced water chestnuts, rinsed and drained	I
I tbsp	cornstarch	15 mL
2 tbsp	water	25 mL
4	green onions, cut in 1-inch (2.5 cm) pieces	4
2 cups	chopped broccoli	500 mL

1. In a large nonstick skillet, heat vegetable and sesame oil if using on medium-high heat. Add beef and cook in batches, stirring, for 5 to 7 minutes, or until browned on all sides. With a slotted spoon, transfer meat to slow cooker stoneware.

2. Add stock, soy sauce, sherry, chili paste, onion, garlic, gingerroot and water chestnuts to slow cooker. Stir well.

3. Cover and cook on **Low** for 8 to 10 hours or on **High** for 4 to 6 hours, or until beef is tender.

4. In a small bowl or jar (page 177), mix together cornstarch and water. Pour into slow cooker along with green onions and broccoli.

5. Cover and cook on **High** for 15 to 20 minutes, or until sauce has thickened and broccoli is tender-crisp.

Gooey Glazed Beef Ribs

Makes 6 servings

A zipped-up sauce slathered over a peppery rub makes these ribs a great summertime treat. No need to stand over a hot barbecue to get great-tasting ribs. Your kitchen can stay cool while the slow cooker does all the work.

Beef short ribs are a perfect cut of beef for the slow cooker. However, they are high in fat, so broil them first to reduce the fat.

• *Slow Cooker Size: 5 to 6 qt*

3 to 4 lbs	meaty beef braising ribs or short ribs	1.5 to 2 kg
1 tsp	black pepper	5 mL
6	cloves garlic, minced	6
1 cup	ketchup	250 mL
½ cup	water	125 mL
½ cup	maple syrup	125 mL
2 tbsp	Worcestershire sauce	25 mL
1 tbsp	Dijon mustard	15 mL

1. Place ribs on a foil-lined baking sheet or broiler pan and sprinkle with pepper. Broil in a preheated oven, 6 inches (15 cm) from heat, turning often, for 10 to 15 minutes, or until browned on both sides. Transfer to a paper towel-lined plate to drain.

2. In a bowl, combine garlic, ketchup, water, maple syrup, Worcestershire and mustard. Place ribs in slow cooker and pour sauce over ribs.

3. Cover and cook on **Low** for 8 to 12 hours or on **High** for 4 to 6 hours, or until tender. Skim any fat from surface of sauce before serving.

East-West Beef Curry

<table>
<tr><td>Makes 6 to
8 servings</td><td colspan="3">• Slow Cooker Size: 3 1/2 to 6 qt</td></tr>
</table>

Fire up your guests with this stew that combines flavors from two different cuisines. Serve with steamed basmati rice (page 73), chutney and/or raisins, chopped peanuts and Indian flatbread (naan). For an extra kick, try using fiery Madras curry powder. Curry powder and naan are both available in Indian food shops.

1 tbsp	vegetable oil	15 mL
2 lbs	stewing beef, cut in 1-inch (2.5 cm) cubes	1 kg
1 tbsp	curry powder	15 mL
1 tbsp	ground coriander	15 mL
1 tsp	ground cumin	5 mL
1 tsp	dry mustard	5 mL
1 1/2 tsp	salt	7 mL
1 tsp	black pepper	5 mL
2	onions, sliced	2
1	red bell pepper, seeded and chopped	1
2	cloves garlic, minced	2
1 tsp	grated lemon zest	5 mL
1	19-oz (540 mL) can stewed tomatoes, with juices	1
1	4 1/2-oz (127 mL) can chopped mild green chilies, including liquid	1
1 cup	beef stock	250 mL
2 tbsp	cider vinegar	25 mL
1 cup	coconut milk	250 mL

1. In a large nonstick skillet, heat oil over medium-high heat. Add beef cubes and cook in batches for 8 to 10 minutes, or until meat is browned on all sides. Return all meat to skillet.

2. Sprinkle meat with curry powder, coriander, cumin, mustard, salt and pepper. Cook, stirring, for 2 minutes. Transfer seasoned meat to slow cooker stoneware.

3. Add onions, red pepper, garlic, lemon zest, tomatoes, green chilies, stock and vinegar to slow cooker. Stir well to combine.

4. Cover and cook on **Low** for 8 to 10 hours or on **High** for 4 to 6 hours, or until beef is tender and stew is bubbling.

5. Stir in coconut milk. Cover and cook on **High** for 5 minutes, or until warmed through.

Mahogany Beef Stew

Makes 6 servings

Grab a cushion and a blanket. This rich and hearty beef stew is perfect for a cozy fireside supper. Serve with horseradish mashed potatoes (page 93).

• *Slow Cooker Size: 3 1/2 to 6 qt*

2 tbsp	all-purpose flour	25 mL
I tsp	dried thyme leaves	5 mL
1/2 tsp	dry mustard	2 mL
1/2 tsp	ground ginger	2 mL
2 lbs	stewing beef, cut in 1-inch (2.5 cm) cubes	I kg
2 tbsp	vegetable oil	25 mL
I cup	dry red wine	250 mL
I	19-oz (540 mL) can Italian-style (page 103) stewed tomatoes, with juices	I
1/3 cup	hoisin sauce	75 mL
3	carrots, peeled and chopped	3
2	parsnips, peeled and chopped	2
I	large onion, chopped	I
2	cloves garlic, minced	2
2	bay leaves	2
	Salt and pepper to taste	
2 tbsp	chopped fresh parsley	25 mL

1. In a large heavy-duty plastic bag, combine flour, thyme, mustard and ginger. In batches, add beef to flour mixture and toss to coat.

2. In a large nonstick skillet, heat 1 tbsp (15 mL) oil over medium-high heat. Cook beef in batches, adding more oil as needed, for 8 to 10 minutes, or until browned on all sides. With a slotted spoon, transfer beef to slow cooker stoneware.

3. Add wine to skillet and bring to a boil, scraping up brown bits stuck to pan. Transfer to slow cooker.

4. Add tomatoes, hoisin sauce, carrots, parsnips, onion, garlic and bay leaves to slow cooker. Stir to combine.

5. Cover and cook on **Low** for 8 to 10 hours or on **High** for 4 to 6 hours, or until meat and vegetables are tender and stew is bubbling. Discard bay leaves. Season with salt and pepper. Serve garnished with fresh parsley.

Mexicali Round Steak

Makes 6 servings

Enjoy this hearty steak with a basket of warmed soft tortillas (page 112). Serve with additional salsa and sprinkle with chopped fresh cilantro.

Vary the taste of this all-in-one meal by using pinto beans instead of black beans. If you wish, use a pre-shredded cheese blend to save a little time.

• *Slow Cooker Size: 3 1/2 to 6 qt*

1 1/2 lbs	outside round marinating beef steak, trimmed	750 g
1/2 tsp	black pepper	2 mL
1 cup	fresh or frozen and defrosted corn kernels	250 mL
1	19-oz (540 mL) can black beans, rinsed and drained, or 2 cups (500 mL) home-cooked beans (page 145)	1
1/2 cup	chopped fresh cilantro	125 mL
2	stalks celery, thinly sliced	2
1	onion, sliced	1
2 cups	salsa	500 mL
1/2 cup	beef stock	125 mL
1 cup	grated Cheddar or Monterey Jack cheese (optional)	250 mL

1. Cut steaks into 6 serving pieces and season with pepper. Place in bottom of slow cooker stoneware. (If using 3 1/2 qt-cooker, steaks will have to be layered.)

2. In a bowl, combine corn, beans, cilantro, celery, onion, salsa and stock. Spoon over beef.

3. Cover and cook on **Low** for 8 to 10 hours or on **High** for 4 to 6 hours, or until beef is tender.

4. Sprinkle with cheese if using. Cover and cook on **High** for 15 to 20 minutes, or until cheese is melted.

Horseradish Mashed Potatoes

Cook and mash 2 lbs (1 kg) peeled potatoes. Stir in 1 cup (250 mL) milk, 2 tbsp (25 mL) butter, 1 minced clove garlic and 2 tbsp (25 mL) creamed horseradish sauce. Makes 6 servings.

Onion Cranberry Brisket

Makes 8 to 10 servings

If you can't find a brisket roast, a cross rib or blade pot roast will work well, too. Serve with lots of garlic mashed potatoes (page 131) and a green vegetable. Use whole berry or jellied cranberry sauce. (You may want to melt the cranberry sauce in the microwave first so it mixes smoothly with the other ingredients.)

• *Slow Cooker Size: 5 to 6 qt*

1	3- to 4-lb (1.5 to 2 kg) beef double brisket, cross rib or blade pot roast	1
1 tbsp	vegetable oil	15 mL
1	14-oz (398 mL) can cranberry sauce	1
1	1½-oz (40 g) envelope onion soup mix	1
2	cloves garlic, minced	2
¼ cup	water	50 mL
2 tbsp	prepared mustard	25 mL
	Salt and black pepper to taste	

1. Cut brisket in half if necessary so it will fit in slow cooker. In a large skillet, heat oil over medium-high heat. Add meat and cook, turning with wooden spoons, for 7 to 10 minutes, or until browned on all sides. Transfer meat to slow cooker stoneware.

2. In a bowl, combine cranberry sauce, onion soup mix, garlic, water and mustard. Mix well and pour over brisket.

3. Cover and cook on **Low** for 10 to 12 hours or on **High** for 6 to 8 hours, or until meat is fork-tender. Transfer brisket to a cutting board.

4. Skim any fat from surface of gravy. Season with salt and pepper. Pour gravy into a sauce boat. Slice roast and arrange on a serving platter. Serve with gravy.

Sauerbraten Beef Stew

Sauerbraten is a German specialty made by marinating beef roast in a sweet-tangy marinade for two to three days. The roast is then browned and simmered in the marinade until it is tender. This slow-cooked version is ready in a fraction of the time it takes to prepare the traditional recipe.

For a traditional German meal, serve this sauerbraten with spätzle, tiny dumplings that often accompany saucy German main dishes.

To make the gingersnap crumbs, process cookies in a food processor or blender or place cookies in a resealable plastic bag. Squeeze all air out of bag and seal. Crush cookies with a rolling pin until crumbs are formed.

• Slow Cooker Size: 3 1/2 to 6 qt

1 tbsp	vegetable oil	15 mL
2 lbs	stewing beef, cut in 1-inch (2.5 cm) cubes	1 kg
1 cup	beef stock, divided	250 mL
2	onions, chopped	2
4	large carrots, peeled and cut in 1-inch (2.5 cm) chunks	4
1/2 cup	cider vinegar	125 mL
1/4 cup	packed brown sugar	50 mL
2	bay leaves	2
1/4 tsp	salt	1 mL
1/4 tsp	black pepper	1 mL
Pinch	ground allspice	Pinch
Pinch	ground cloves	Pinch
1/2 cup	gingersnap cookie crumbs	125 mL
1 cup	frozen and defrosted chopped green beans (optional)	250 mL
1/4 cup	raisins (optional)	50 mL
2 tbsp	chopped fresh parsley	25 mL

1. In a large nonstick skillet, heat oil over medium-high heat. Cook beef in batches for about 8 to 10 minutes, or until browned all over. With a slotted spoon, transfer beef to slow cooker stoneware.

2. Add 1/2 cup (125 mL) stock to skillet and bring to a boil, scraping up any brown bits in bottom of pan. Transfer stock mixture to slow cooker. Stir in remaining stock, onions, carrots, vinegar, brown sugar, bay leaves, salt, pepper, allspice and cloves.

3. Cover and cook on **Low** for 8 to 10 hours or on **High** for 4 to 6 hours, or until meat and carrots are tender and stew is bubbling. Discard bay leaves.

4. Add gingersnaps, green beans and raisins if using. Cover and cook on **High** for 20 minutes, or until beans are tender. Sprinkle with parsley.

Nancy's Rouladen

Makes 8 to 10 servings

This tasty dish comes courtesy of my friend Nancy Forte. She says it originated in an old church cookbook but has been adapted over the years. She always serves it with mashed potatoes (pages 93 and 131) and a green vegetable. Use garlic-flavored dill pickles if you have them.

If the steak slices are large once they have been flattened, cut the rolls in half before adding to the slow cooker. Each roll should be about 4 inches (10 cm) long.

Mushroom and Green Pepper Rouladen
Omit dill pickle. After cooking bacon, cook 1 cup (250 mL) finely chopped mushrooms and ½ cup (125 mL) finely chopped green pepper in bacon drippings. Add to filling when assembling rolls.

• *Slow Cooker Size: 3½ to 6 qt*

2 lbs	rouladen or inside round steak, cut in 8 to 10 slices	1 kg
1 lb	bacon, finely chopped	500 g
8	cloves garlic, minced	8
½ cup	Dijon mustard	125 mL
1	sweet onion, finely chopped	1
1 cup	finely chopped dill pickle	250 mL
2 tbsp	vegetable oil	25 mL
	Water	

GRAVY
¼ cup	all-purpose flour	50 mL
¼ cup	water	50 mL
1 tbsp	Worcestershire sauce	15 mL
	Salt and black pepper to taste	

1. With a mallet, pound steak slices until about ⅛ inch (3 mm) thick. Cut off uneven ends if necessary.

2. In a large nonstick skillet over medium-high heat, cook bacon, stirring occasionally, for 8 to 10 minutes, or until tender but not crisp. Drain and cool. Discard fat from pan.

3. Lay beef slices on cutting board and rub each with about ½ tsp (2 mL) minced garlic. Spread each slice with a heaping teaspoon Dijon mustard. Sprinkle with cooked bacon, onion and pickle, keeping filling about ½ inch (1 cm) from edge of meat.

4. Starting at narrow end, roll up each slice, encasing filling. Secure each roll with toothpick.

Italian Stuffed Peppers (page 108)
Overleaf: Ginger Pork Wraps (page 112)

5. Add 1 tbsp (15 mL) oil to skillet and heat over medium-high heat. Add rolls and cook in batches for about 5 minutes, or until browned on all sides, adding more oil as needed. Transfer to slow cooker stoneware, seam side down. Pour in enough water to cover rolls.

6. Cover and cook on **Low** for 8 to 10 hours or on **High** for 4 to 6 hours, or until tender. With a slotted spoon, carefully remove rolls to a platter and keep warm.

7. To make gravy, strain 2 cups (500 mL) cooking liquid from slow cooker into a saucepan. (Discard remaining liquid.)

8. In a bowl, whisk together flour and water until smooth. Whisk into saucepan. Bring to a boil over high heat, whisking constantly, for 5 to 7 minutes, or until thickened. Add Worcestershire, salt and pepper.

9. Pour sauce over rolls on platter or serve separately in a sauceboat.

Sweet Onions

Sweet onions such as Vidalia, Maui, Rio and Walla Walla are juicy and mild. Or try Texan 1015 onions if you can find them. They are wonderfully sweet and especially good for French onion soup. If you can't find any of these varieties, use Spanish or red onions.

Key West Ribs (page 113)

Barbecued Beef Sandwiches

Makes 8 servings

Hot sandwiches don't come any easier. Just combine the sauce ingredients and pour over the meat in the slow cooker. Be sure to toast the sandwich buns to help keep them from getting soggy. You can also serve the beef on its own as a roast.

Do not use diet cola in this recipe. It will impart a strange aftertaste.

Liquid smoke is exactly that — liquid mixed with smoke. Brushed on or stirred into food, it lends a smoky, hickory flavor to dishes. Look for it in the condiment aisle of the supermarket.

• *Slow Cooker Size: 3 1/2 to 6 qt*

1	3- to 4-lb (1.5 to 2 kg) beef cross rib or blade roast	1
1 tsp	salt	5 mL
1/2 tsp	black pepper	2 mL
1 tbsp	vegetable oil	15 mL
2 cups	ketchup	500 mL
1	12-oz (355 mL) can cola	1
1/4 cup	Worcestershire sauce	50 mL
2 tbsp	prepared mustard	25 mL
2 tbsp	liquid smoke	25 mL
1/4 tsp	hot red pepper sauce or 1 jalapeño pepper, seeded and finely chopped	1 mL
8	kaiser buns, toasted	8

1. Season roast on all sides with salt and pepper.

2. In a large skillet, heat oil over medium-high heat. Add meat and cook, turning with a wooden spoon, for 7 to 10 minutes, or until browned on all sides. Transfer meat to slow cooker stoneware.

3. In a bowl, combine ketchup, cola, Worcestershire, mustard, liquid smoke and hot pepper sauce. Pour sauce over roast.

4. Cover and cook on **Low** for 10 to 12 hours or on **High** for 4 to 6 hours, or until meat is fork-tender.

5. Remove meat from slow cooker and let stand for 10 minutes before carving. Skim fat from sauce. Place meat on a kaiser bun, add 1 tbsp (15 mL) sauce and cover with remaining half of bun. Serve with additional sauce for dipping.

Easy-on-Ya Lasagna

Makes 6 to 8 servings

This easy slow cooker version of lasagna is another contribution from my neighbor Caroline Wolff. It tastes as good as the baked version but is a lot less work.

You can substitute mild Italian sausage for the ground beef. Reduce the basil and oregano to ¼ tsp (1 mL) each.

• *Slow Cooker Size: 3½ to 6 qt*

8	dried lasagna noodles, broken in bite-sized pieces	8
1½ lbs	lean ground beef	750 g
1	onion, finely chopped	1
2	cloves garlic, minced	2
1	28-oz (796 mL) can tomatoes, chopped, with juices	1
2 tbsp	tomato paste	25 mL
2 tsp	granulated sugar	10 mL
2 tbsp	chopped fresh parsley	25 mL
½ tsp	dried basil leaves	2 mL
½ tsp	dried oregano leaves	2 mL
1 cup	creamed cottage cheese	250 mL
2 cups	grated mozzarella cheese	500 mL
½ tsp	black pepper	2 mL
½ cup	grated Parmesan cheese	125 mL

1. In a large pot of boiling salted water, cook noodles for 5 to 7 minutes, or until softened but slightly undercooked. Drain and rinse under cold water.

2. In a large nonstick skillet over medium-high heat, cook ground beef, onion and garlic, breaking up meat with a spoon, for 7 minutes, or until beef is no longer pink. With a slotted spoon, transfer meat mixture to slow cooker stoneware.

3. In a bowl, combine tomatoes, tomato paste, sugar, parsley, basil and oregano. Add to slow cooker along with cottage cheese, mozzarella, pepper and partially cooked noodles. Stir well.

4. Cover and cook on **Low** for 6 to 8 hours or on **High** for 3 to 4 hours, or until hot and bubbling.

5. Sprinkle with Parmesan cheese. Cover and cook on **High** for 10 minutes, or until cheese has melted.

Tortilla Stack

Makes 4 to 6 servings

Enchiladas are a Mexican specialty consisting of tortillas rolled around a meat, vegetable or cheese filling. The tortillas are heated and topped with tomato sauce and cheese. I have simplified things a bit in this recipe, where the tortillas are simply layered with seasoned meat filling, beans, cheese and sour cream.

Serve this casserole with sliced fresh tomatoes or a green salad tossed with radishes and orange segments.

You can substitute 1½ cups (375 mL) shredded cooked chicken for the ground beef.

Pickled jalapeños can be found in the Mexican food section of the supermarket.

• Slow Cooker Size: 5 to 6 qt

1½ lbs	lean ground beef	750 g
1	onion, finely chopped	1
4	cloves garlic, minced	4
4 tsp	chili powder	20 mL
½ tsp	dried oregano leaves	2 mL
¼ tsp	salt	1 mL
Pinch	cayenne pepper	Pinch
1	19-oz (540 mL) can red kidney or black beans, rinsed and drained, or 2 cups (500 mL) home-cooked beans (page 145)	1
1 cup	fresh or frozen and defrosted corn kernels	250 mL
1 cup	salsa, divided	250 mL
4	10-inch (25 cm) corn or flour tortillas	4
1 cup	grated Cheddar cheese, divided	250 mL
2 tbsp	pickled jalapeño slices	25 mL
½ cup	sour cream	125 mL

1. In a large nonstick skillet, cook ground beef, onion and garlic over medium-high heat, breaking up meat with the back of a spoon, for 5 to 7 minutes, or until meat is no longer pink.

2. Add chili powder, oregano, salt and cayenne to skillet and cook, stirring, for 2 minutes.

3. In a bowl, mash kidney beans. Stir in corn and ¼ cup (50 mL) salsa.

4. Lay one tortilla in bottom of lightly greased slow cooker stoneware. Spread one-third of beef mixture over tortilla, then one-third of salsa/bean mixture, one-quarter of cheese and one-third of jalapeño slices. Repeat layers twice. Top with remaining tortilla and spread remaining salsa over top.

5. Cover and cook on **High** for 2 to 3 hours, or until heated through.

6. Spread sour cream over tortillas and sprinkle with remaining cheese.

7. Cover and cook on **High** for 15 minutes, or until cheese melts.

8. Let stand for 10 minutes before serving. Remove from slow cooker with a spatula and slice.

Frozen Vegetables

In general, you should defrost frozen vegetables before adding them to the slow cooker. Adding them while still frozen will bring down the cooking temperature of the dish. Defrost overnight in the refrigerator or rinse under cold running water to separate and drain well.

Chili Spaghetti Pie

Makes 6 to 8 servings

Spaghetti pie originated as a creative use for leftover cooked spaghetti. This pie combines two family favorites — spaghetti and chili.

The beans in this recipe are an excellent source of soluble fiber.

• *Slow Cooker Size: 5 to 6 qt*

CRUST

8 oz	dried spaghetti	250 g
1	egg, lightly beaten	1
¼ cup	butter, melted	50 mL
⅓ cup	grated Parmesan cheese	75 mL
1 tsp	chili powder	5 mL

FILLING

1 lb	lean ground beef	500 g
1	onion, finely chopped	1
1	14-oz (398 mL) can baked beans in tomato sauce	1
1	19-oz (540 mL) Italian-style stewed tomatoes, with juices	1
1 tsp	chili powder	5 mL
½ tsp	black pepper	2 mL
2 cups	grated Monterey Jack cheese, divided	500 mL

1. To prepare crust, cook spaghetti in a pot of boiling salted water for 6 to 8 minutes, or until almost tender but still firm. Drain and rinse well under cold water.

2. In a large bowl, combine egg, melted butter, Parmesan and chili powder. Add cooked spaghetti and toss to coat. Spoon into lightly greased slow cooker stoneware, pushing mixture slightly up sides of stoneware.

3. To prepare filling, in a large nonstick skillet over medium-high heat, cook ground beef and onion, breaking up meat with back of spoon, for 5 to 7 minutes, or until meat is no longer pink. Drain off any fat.

Make Ahead

This dish can be completely assembled up to 24 hours before cooking. Chill crust and filling separately before assembling dish. Refrigerate overnight in slow cooker stoneware. The next day, place stoneware in slow cooker and continue to cook as directed.

4. Add beans, tomatoes, chili powder and pepper to skillet. Cook, stirring, for 2 minutes, or until thoroughly heated. Stir in 1 cup (250 mL) cheese.

5. Spoon meat/bean mixture into spaghetti-lined stoneware.

6. Cover and cook on **Low** for 4 to 6 hours, or until hot and bubbly.

7. Sprinkle remaining cheese over top of pie. Cover and cook on **High** for 20 to 30 minutes, or until cheese melts.

Cooking Ground Meat in the Slow Cooker

Always make sure ground meat is fully cooked before adding it to the slow cooker. Cold uncooked ground meat takes too long to come to a safe temperature. (Cooking and draining the meat first also helps to eliminate extra fat and the liquid that accumulates during cooking.)

Italian-style Tomatoes

In place of one 19-oz (540 mL) can Italian-style stewed tomatoes, use regular stewed tomatoes and add ½ tsp (2 mL) dried Italian herb seasoning or a combination of dried basil, oregano and thyme (page 36).

Barbecued Beef Chili

Makes 10 to 12 servings

This recipe is meant to feed a crowd of hungry people, providing at least ten hearty servings. It's the perfect dish to prepare for a football or skating party. For extra heat, add more cayenne.

Any beans can be used in place of Great Northern or white kidney beans. Try pinto, red kidney or black beans.

Make Ahead

This dish can be made a day ahead. In fact, letting it sit for 24 hours enhances the flavors. Cook meat, shred and cool completely before returning meat to slow cooker. Refrigerate overnight. The next day, add beans and cook on **High** for 1 to 2 hours, or until hot and bubbling.

- *Slow Cooker Size: 5 to 6 qt*

2 tbsp	chili powder	25 mL
1 tbsp	garlic powder	15 mL
2 tsp	celery seed	10 mL
1 tsp	black pepper	5 mL
1/4 tsp	cayenne pepper	1 mL
1	boneless beef pot roast, cross rib, rump or brisket (about 3 to 4 lbs/1.5 to 2 kg)	1
1	small onion, chopped	1
2 cups	tomato-based chili sauce	500 mL
1 cup	ketchup	250 mL
1/2 cup	barbecue sauce	125 mL
1/3 cup	packed brown sugar	75 mL
1/4 cup	cider vinegar	50 mL
1/4 cup	Worcestershire sauce	50 mL
1 tsp	dry mustard	5 mL
2	19-oz (540 mL) cans Great Northern or white kidney beans, rinsed and drained, or 4 cups (1 L) home-cooked beans (page 145)	2

1. In a small bowl, combine chili powder, garlic powder, celery seed, black pepper and cayenne.

2. Cut roast into four smaller portions and rub seasoning mixture on all sides of chunks. Place in slow cooker stoneware.

3. In a bowl, combine onion, chili sauce, ketchup, barbecue sauce, brown sugar, vinegar, Worcestershire and mustard. Pour over meat.

4. Cover and cook on **Low** for 8 to 10 hours or on **High** for 4 to 5 hours, or until meat is fork-tender.

5. With a slotted spoon, transfer meat chunks to a large bowl. Using two forks, shred meat.

6. Skim fat from sauce. Return shredded meat to slow cooker and add beans. Cover and cook on **Low** for 1 hour, or until heated through.

Pepperoni Pizza Chili

Makes 6 to 8 servings

All the kids' favorite ingredients rolled into a pot of chili! Serve with Italian bread and a Caesar salad.

You can substitute equal amounts of lean ground turkey or chicken for the ground beef. You can also use a blend of pre-shredded pizza cheese in place of the mozzarella.

If your kids love Italian food but prefer it plain, omit the mushrooms and red pepper and serve them as toppings for the adults.

Make Ahead

This dish can be completely assembled up to 24 hours before cooking. Chill cooked meat and vegetables separately. Then assemble dish and refrigerate overnight in slow cooker stoneware. The next day, place stoneware in slow cooker and continue to cook as directed.

• *Slow Cooker Size: 3¹/₂ to 6 qt*

1 lb	lean ground beef	500 g
2	cloves garlic, minced	2
1	19-oz (540 mL) can pinto or Romano beans, rinsed and drained, or 2 cups (500 mL) home-cooked beans (page 145)	1
1	7¹/₂-oz (213 mL) can pizza sauce	1
1	19-oz (540 mL) can Italian-style (page 103) stewed tomatoes, with juices	1
1	7¹/₂-oz (213 mL) can tomato sauce	1
4 oz	pepperoni, sliced	125 g
1 cup	sliced mushrooms	250 mL
1	red bell pepper, seeded and finely chopped	1
1 tsp	dried Italian herb seasoning (page 36)	5 mL
¹/₂ tsp	salt	2 mL
¹/₂ cup	grated mozzarella cheese	125 mL

1. In a large nonstick skillet, cook beef and garlic over medium-high heat, breaking up beef with back of a spoon, for 5 to 7 minutes, or until beef is no longer pink. With a slotted spoon, transfer meat to slow cooker stoneware.

2. Add beans, pizza sauce, tomatoes, tomato sauce, pepperoni, mushrooms, red pepper, Italian seasoning and salt to slow cooker and stir in.

3. Cover and cook on **Low** for 8 to 10 hours or on **High** for 4 to 5 hours, or until hot and bubbling.

4. Spoon chili into individual serving bowls and top with mozzarella cheese.

Rock'n and Roast'n Chili

Makes 6 to 8 servings

Red alert! For those who like a little kick to their meal, this meaty beef chili will knock the socks off anyone who can take it. A loaf of crusty bread is a must, along with a few cold beers.

• *Slow Cooker Size: 3½ to 6 qt*

2 tbsp	vegetable oil	25 mL
2 lbs	stewing beef, cut in 1-inch (2.5 cm) cubes	1 kg
2 tbsp	chili powder	25 mL
Pinch	ground cumin	Pinch
½ cup	chopped drained pickled hot banana peppers (stems and seeds removed)	125 mL
1	onion, chopped	1
3	cloves garlic, minced	3
1	fresh jalapeño or banana pepper, seeded and chopped	1
1	19-oz (540 mL) can Italian-style (page 103) stewed tomatoes, with juices	1
1	5½-oz (156 mL) can tomato paste	1
1	19-oz (540 mL) can red kidney beans, rinsed and drained, or 2 cups (500 mL) home-cooked beans (page 145)	1
1	4½-oz (127 mL) can chopped mild green chilies, including liquid	1
1 tsp	hot red pepper sauce	5 mL
1 tsp	salt	5 mL

1. In a large nonstick skillet, heat 1 tbsp (15 mL) oil over medium-high heat. Add beef cubes in batches and cook, stirring, for 8 to 10 minutes, or until browned on all sides, adding more oil as needed. Return all beef to skillet

2. Add chili powder and cumin to skillet and cook, stirring, for 1 minute. With a slotted spoon, transfer meat to slow cooker stoneware.

3. Add chopped pickled peppers, onion, garlic, jalapeño, tomatoes, tomato paste, beans, green chilies, hot pepper sauce and salt to slow cooker and stir in.

4. Cover and cook on **Low** for 8 to 10 hours or on **High** for 4 to 6 hours, or until meat is tender and stew is hot and bubbling. Taste and add more hot pepper sauce if desired.

Hearty Veal Stew with Red Wine and Sweet Peppers

Makes 6 servings

In this Italian-inspired stew, chunks of veal cook in a rich tomato sauce seasoned with garlic and sage. Capers lend a tangy contrast to the sweet bell peppers. Serve over egg noodles with a bottle of red wine.

• Slow Cooker Size: 3 1/2 to 6 qt

1/4 cup	all-purpose flour	50 mL
1 tsp	salt	5 mL
1/2 tsp	black pepper	2 mL
2 lbs	veal stewing meat, cut in 1-inch (2.5 cm) cubes	1 kg
2 tbsp	vegetable oil	25 mL
2 tbsp	butter	25 mL
3	cloves garlic, peeled and crushed	3
3/4 cup	dry red wine	175 mL
1	19-oz (540 mL) can Italian-style (page 103) stewed tomatoes, with juices	1
1 tsp	dried sage leaves	5 mL
2	red bell peppers, seeded and cut in 1/2-inch (1 cm) pieces	2
2 tbsp	drained capers	25 mL

1. In a large heavy-duty plastic bag, combine flour, salt and pepper. In batches, add veal to flour mixture and toss to coat.

2. In a large nonstick skillet, heat 1 tbsp (15 mL) oil and 1 tbsp (15 mL) butter over medium-high heat. Add garlic. Cook, stirring, for 1 minute. Transfer to slow cooker stoneware with a slotted spoon.

3. Add veal to skillet in batches and cook for 6 minutes, or until browned on all sides, adding more oil and butter as needed. Transfer veal to slow cooker with a slotted spoon.

4. Add wine to skillet. Bring to a boil, scraping up any browned bits from bottom of pan. Transfer to slow cooker. Add tomatoes and sage to slow cooker and stir to combine.

5. Cover and cook on **Low** for 8 to 10 hours or on **High** for 4 to 6 hours, or until meat is tender.

6. Add peppers and capers. Cover and cook on **High** for 15 to 20 minutes, or until heated through.

Italian Stuffed Peppers

Makes 6 servings

Stuffed peppers are a classic slow cooker meal. They are quick and easy to prepare, and this recipe will be a welcome addition to your family's repertoire. It is best to use an oval slow cooker so that the peppers fit in one layer.

Cutting a hole in the bottom of the peppers allows moisture and steam to penetrate, promoting even cooking.

You can substitute ground turkey or chicken for the veal, but increase the pepper to $\frac{1}{2}$ tsp (2 mL).

• *Slow Cooker Size: 6 qt*

6	small to medium red, yellow and/or green bell peppers, tops removed, cored and seeded	6
1 lb	lean ground veal	500 g
1½ cups	cooked rice (about ½ cup/125 mL uncooked)	375 mL
2	eggs, lightly beaten	2
2	cloves garlic, minced	2
⅓ cup	grated Parmesan cheese	75 mL
2 tbsp	finely chopped fresh parsley	25 mL
½ tsp	salt	2 mL
¼ tsp	black pepper	1 mL
1 cup	tomato sauce or pasta sauce	250 mL

1. Cut a small hole in the bottom of each pepper.

2. In a bowl, combine veal, rice, eggs, garlic, Parmesan, parsley, salt and pepper. Spoon meat mixture into peppers. Do not pack down.

3. Stand peppers upright in slow cooker stoneware. Spoon tomato sauce evenly over top of each stuffed pepper.

4. Cover and cook on **Low** for 4 to 5 hours, or until peppers are tender and a meat thermometer reads 170°F (77°C).

Pork and Lamb

Cider Pork Stew

Makes 6 servings

The tang of the vinegar and sweetness of the onion blend well in this easy-to-assemble dinner. Serve with garlic mashed potatoes (page 131) or steamed rice (page 73).

Orange Fennel Pork Stew
Replace thyme with 2 tsp (10 mL) crushed fennel seeds. Replace apple cider with 1 cup (250 mL) orange juice concentrate. Add 2 tbsp (25 mL) grated gingerroot to slow cooker with peppers. Omit bay leaves and garnish with orange slices instead of apple.

• Slow Cooker Size: 3 1/2 to 6 qt

2	onions, sliced	2
4	cloves garlic, minced	4
1/3 cup	all-purpose flour	75 mL
1 tbsp	dried thyme leaves	15 mL
1 tsp	salt	5 mL
1/2 tsp	black pepper	2 mL
4 lbs	boneless pork shoulder butt roast, trimmed of excess fat, cut in 1-inch (2.5 cm) cubes	2 kg
1/4 cup	vegetable oil	50 mL
1 cup	apple cider	250 mL
1/4 cup	cider vinegar	50 mL
2	bay leaves	2
2	red bell peppers, seeded and coarsely chopped	2
1	red apple, unpeeled, thinly sliced	1
1 tbsp	chopped fresh parsley	15 mL

1. Place onions and garlic in slow cooker stoneware.

2. In a large heavy-duty plastic bag, combine flour, thyme, salt and pepper. Add pork in batches and toss to coat.

3. In a large nonstick skillet, heat 2 tbsp (25 mL) oil over medium-high heat. Cook pork in batches, adding oil as needed, for 8 to 10 minutes, or until browned on all sides. Transfer pork to slow cooker.

4. Add apple cider and vinegar to skillet and bring to a boil, scraping up any brown bits on bottom of pan. Pour over pork in slow cooker. Add bay leaves.

5. Cover and cook on **Low** for 8 to 10 hours or on **High** for 3 to 4 hours, or until pork is tender.

6. Stir in peppers. Cover and cook on **High** for 1 hour. Discard bay leaves. Skim fat from sauce. Taste and adjust seasonings if necessary. Serve topped with apple slices and parsley.

Double Decker Spicy Pork Tacos

Makes 6 servings

Tacos are Mexican-style sandwiches filled with meat, beans, cheese, lettuce, onions, salsa and guacamole. In this recipe, soft flour tortillas prevent the filling from falling out of the crispy taco shells — a common hazard when you are eating tacos! Add any extra toppings you wish.

• *Slow Cooker Size: 3 1/2 to 6 qt*

1	2-lb (1 kg) boneless pork loin rib end roast, trimmed of excess fat	1
1 tbsp	chili powder	15 mL
1/4 tsp	ground cumin	1 mL
1/4 tsp	hot red pepper flakes	1 mL
1	19-oz (540 mL) can tomatoes, drained and chopped	1
1	4 1/2-oz (127 mL) can chopped mild green chilies, including liquid	1
1	14-oz (398 mL) can refried beans	1
12	6-inch (15 cm) flour tortillas	12
12	taco shells	12
3/4 cup	grated Cheddar cheese	175 mL
1 1/2 cups	shredded lettuce	375 mL

1. Place pork roast in slow cooker stoneware. Sprinkle chili powder, cumin and hot pepper flakes over roast. Add tomatoes and green chilies.

2. Cover and cook on **Low** for 8 to 10 hours or on **High** for 4 to 5 hours, or until pork is tender.

3. Transfer pork to a bowl and shred meat using two forks. Skim fat from sauce. Return meat to sauce in slow cooker.

4. Heat refried beans, tortillas and taco shells according to package directions.

5. Spread flour tortillas with a spoonful of hot refried beans. Set 1 taco shell in center. Fold flour tortilla around taco shell.

6. Spoon about 1/3 cup (75 mL) pork mixture into each taco shell. Top with cheese and lettuce.

Ginger Pork Wraps

Makes 6 servings

These wraps combine the flavors of sweet and sour pork with crisp vegetables. Everyone will be asking for seconds.

If you are pressed for time, look for pre-packaged coleslaw mix to use in place of the cabbage and carrot (use about 3½ cups/875 mL).

• *Slow Cooker Size: 3½ to 6 qt*

¼ cup	hoisin sauce	50 mL
3 tbsp	grated gingerroot	45 mL
3 tbsp	liquid honey	45 mL
1	2½-lb (1.25 kg) boneless pork loin rib end roast, trimmed of excess fat	1
2½ cups	shredded cabbage	625 mL
½ cup	shredded carrot	125 mL
3	green onions, finely chopped	3
2 tbsp	rice vinegar	25 mL
10 to 12	10-inch (25 cm) flour tortillas	10 to 12

1. In a bowl, combine hoisin sauce, gingerroot and honey.

2. Place pork roast in slow cooker stoneware and brush with sauce to coat completely.

3. Cover and cook on **Low** for 8 to 10 hours or on **High** for 4 to 5 hours, or until meat is very tender.

4. Transfer pork to a bowl and pull meat apart in shreds using two forks. Skim fat from sauce. Return meat to slow cooker.

5. In a bowl, combine cabbage, carrot, green onions and vinegar.

6. Wrap tortillas in foil and heat in a preheated 350°F (180°C) oven for 10 minutes.

7. To serve, spread about ⅓ cup (75 mL) pork mixture down center of each warm tortilla. Top with ¼ cup (50 mL) cabbage mixture. Roll up each tortilla tightly.

Hoisin Sauce

Hoisin sauce is used extensively in Chinese cuisine, both in cooking and as a condiment. Made from soybeans, garlic and chilies, the thick red-brown sauce has a sweet, spicy flavor.

Key West Ribs

Makes 6 servings

For a taste of the tropics in the middle of winter, make a batch of these meaty ribs.

Country-style ribs are the meatiest variety of pork ribs. They are cut from the loin so they tend to have less fat than side or back ribs. If you can't find country-style ribs, side or back ribs will also work in this recipe. Broil them for 8 to 10 minutes on each side before placing them in the slow cooker.

• *Slow Cooker Size: 3 1/2 to 6 qt*

3 lbs	country-style pork ribs, cut in individual ribs	1.5 kg
1	onion, finely chopped	1
1/4 cup	barbecue sauce	50 mL
1 tsp	grated orange zest	5 mL
1 tsp	grated lime zest	5 mL
	Juice of 1 orange (about 1/4 cup/50 mL)	
	Juice of 1 lime (about 2 tbsp/25 mL)	
2 tbsp	cornstarch	25 mL
2 tbsp	cold water	25 mL
	Salt and black pepper to taste	

1. Place ribs on a foil-lined broiler pan or baking sheet. Place about 6 inches (15 cm) from preheated broiler element. Broil, turning often, for 10 to 15 minutes, or until browned on all sides. Transfer to a paper towel-lined plate to drain. Transfer to slow cooker stoneware.

2. In a bowl, combine onion, barbecue sauce, orange and lime zest and orange and lime juice. Pour over ribs.

3. Cover and cook on **Low** for 6 to 8 hours or on **High** for 3 to 4 hours, or until pork is tender.

4. Transfer ribs to a platter and keep warm. Skim fat from sauce.

5. In a small bowl or jar (page 177), dissolve cornstarch in cold water and whisk into sauce. Cover and cook on **High** for 10 minutes, or until thickened. Season with salt and pepper.

Fresh Gingerroot

There is no need to peel gingerroot before grating. Use a standard kitchen grater with fine holes. Wrap any unused ginger in plastic wrap and freeze. Frozen gingerroot can be grated without defrosting.

Hawaiian Pork Stew

**Makes 4 to
6 servings**

Serve this with a
tropical fruit plate and
fragrant rice (page 73).
Use bright orange yams
in this recipe. They
are sweeter, moister
and more colorful
than the pale yellow
sweet potatoes.

• *Slow Cooker Size: 3 1/2 to 6 qt*		
3 tbsp	all-purpose flour	45 mL
I tsp	salt	5 mL
I tsp	black pepper	5 mL
1/2 tsp	ground cinnamon	2 mL
1/4 tsp	dried oregano leaves	I mL
1/4 tsp	ground cloves	I mL
2 lbs	boneless pork shoulder butt roast, cut in I-inch (2.5 cm) cubes	I kg
2 tbsp	vegetable oil	25 mL
I cup	chicken stock	250 mL
I	onion, chopped	I
2	cloves garlic, minced	2
I	19-oz (540 mL) can tomatoes, chopped, with juices	I
I	large sweet potato, peeled and cubed	I
I tbsp	packed brown sugar	15 mL
I cup	fresh or canned pineapple chunks	250 mL
1/4 cup	sliced pimento-stuffed green olives	50 mL
1/2	green bell pepper, seeded and chopped	1/2
1/4 cup	chopped fresh parsley	50 mL

1. In a large heavy-duty plastic bag, combine flour, salt, pepper, cinnamon, oregano and cloves. Add pork cubes in batches and coat with flour mixture.

2. In a large nonstick skillet, heat 1 tbsp (15 mL) oil over medium-high heat. Cook pork in batches, adding more oil as needed, for 5 to 7 minutes, or until browned on all sides. With a slotted spoon, transfer pork to slow cooker stoneware.

3. Add stock to skillet. Bring to a boil, stirring to scrape up any browned bits from bottom of pan. Transfer to slow cooker.

4. Add onion, garlic, tomatoes, sweet potato and brown sugar to slow cooker and stir in.

5. Cover and cook on **Low** for 8 to 10 hours or on **High** for 4 to 6 hours, or until meat and potatoes are tender and stew is bubbling.

6. Stir in pineapple chunks, olives, green pepper and parsley.

7. Cover and cook on **High** for 15 to 20 minutes, or until heated through.

Garlic

Chopped garlic in the jar is a convenient alternative to fresh garlic. It's easy to use and will keep in the refrigerator for up to six months.

Slow and Easy Barbecued Ribs

Makes 6 servings

While many of us think of a grill as a barbecue, those in the Carolinas know that an authentic barbecue means slow cooking pork with a "mop" or top-secret sauce over a smoldering fire. This recipe uses the same principle and cooks meaty ribs slowly in a rich, savory barbecue sauce. Serve with coleslaw (page 57), pickles and cornbread.

- *Slow Cooker Size: 3 1/2 to 6 qt*

3 lbs	country-style pork ribs, cut in individual ribs	1.5 kg
1	large onion, chopped	1
1/2 cup	finely chopped celery	125 mL
3/4 cup	ketchup	175 mL
1/4 cup	apple juice	50 mL
1/4 cup	water	50 mL
2 tbsp	lemon juice	25 mL
2 tbsp	packed brown sugar	25 mL
1 tbsp	dry mustard	15 mL
1 tbsp	cider vinegar	15 mL
1 tbsp	Worcestershire sauce	15 mL
2 tsp	paprika	10 mL
1 tbsp	prepared horseradish	15 mL

1. Place ribs on a foil-lined broiler pan or baking sheet. Place 6 inches (15 cm) from preheated broiler element. Broil, turning often, for 10 to 15 minutes, or until browned on all sides. Transfer to a paper towel-lined plate to drain. Transfer ribs to slow cooker stoneware.

2. In a bowl, combine onion, celery, ketchup, apple juice, water, lemon juice, brown sugar, mustard, vinegar, Worcestershire and paprika. Pour sauce over ribs.

3. Cover and cook on **Low** for 6 to 8 hours or on **High** for 3 to 4 hours, or until pork is tender.

4. Transfer ribs to a serving platter and keep warm. Skim fat from sauce and stir in horseradish. For a thicker sauce, transfer to a saucepan and bring to a boil. Simmer gently, stirring often, until sauce is desired consistency.

5. Serve sauce over ribs or on the side for dipping.

Slow Cooker-to-Grill Sticky Ribs

Makes 4 servings

This is a great way to use your slow cooker in the hot summer months, without heating up the kitchen.

Make Ahead
Prepare these succulent ribs the night before and let them cook in the slow cooker while you are sleeping. Refrigerate the ribs the next morning in the sticky sauce. They will be ready to throw on the grill at the end of the day.

• *Slow Cooker Size: 3 1/2 to 6 qt*

4 lbs	pork back ribs, trimmed of excess fat, cut in serving-sized portions	2 kg
1	onion, sliced	1
1	stalk celery, with leaves	1
2	cloves garlic, peeled and crushed	2
2	bay leaves	2
1 tsp	whole black peppercorns	5 mL

STICKY SAUCE

1/2 cup	barbecue sauce	125 mL
1/2 cup	grape jelly	125 mL
2	cloves garlic, minced	2
Dash	hot red pepper sauce	Dash

1. Place ribs in slow cooker stoneware. (For smaller slow cookers, ribs may have to be cut into smaller portions to fit.)

2. Place onion, celery, garlic, bay leaves and peppercorns around ribs. Cover with water.

3. Cover and cook on **Low** for 6 to 8 hours, or until tender. Transfer ribs to a bowl. Discard cooking liquid and vegetables.

4. To prepare sauce, in a saucepan over medium heat, combine barbecue sauce, grape jelly, minced garlic and hot pepper sauce. Cook for 5 minutes, stirring constantly, until jelly has melted.

5. Preheat barbecue and carefully oil grill rack. Brush ribs generously with sauce. Grill ribs over low heat 4 to 6 inches (10 to 15 cm) from coals. Grill for 15 to 20 minutes, or until browned, turning occasionally and brushing with sauce. Discard any remaining sauce.

Honey and Spice Glazed Pork Chops

Makes 4 servings		

The best chops to buy for the slow cooker are thick-cut loin chops from the rib end or shoulder butt chops. Avoid center-cut loin chops as they will cook too quickly and dry out.

• *Slow Cooker Size: 3 1/2 to 6 qt*

1/4 cup	liquid honey	50 mL
2 tbsp	Dijon mustard	25 mL
1/2 tsp	ground ginger	2 mL
1/4 tsp	ground cinnamon	1 mL
Pinch	ground cloves	Pinch
1 tbsp	vegetable oil	15 mL
4	pork loin rib end chops or shoulder butt chops, 1 inch (2.5 cm) thick, trimmed of excess fat	4
1/2 tsp	salt	2 mL
1/4 tsp	black pepper	1 mL
2 tbsp	cornstarch	25 mL
2 tbsp	water	25 mL

1. In a small bowl, combine honey, mustard, ginger, cinnamon and cloves.

2. In a large nonstick skillet, heat oil over medium-high heat. Sprinkle chops with salt and pepper and cook in batches for about 5 minutes per side, or until brown.

3. Transfer chops to slow cooker stoneware. Pour honey-mustard sauce mixture over chops.

4. Cover and cook loin rib end chops on **Low** for 4 to 5 hours or on **High** for 2 to 3 hours, or until pork is tender. (Shoulder butt chops should cook on **Low** for 6 to 8 hours or on **High** for 3 to 4 hours.) With a slotted spoon, remove pork to a platter. Cover to keep warm.

5. In a small bowl or jar (page 177), combine cornstarch and water. Stir into sauce in slow cooker.

6. Cover and cook on **High** for 15 to 20 minutes, or until thickened. Pour over chops and serve.

Pork Chops with Curried Apple Onion Sauce

The curry flavor goes well with the pork and fruit in this dish.

You can substitute ¼ cup (50 mL) evaporated milk for the cream. Freeze leftover evaporated milk in ice cube trays to make it easy to add small amounts to pasta sauces and soups.

If you wish, you can puree the sauce in a blender or food processor (or use an immersion blender) before spooning it over the chops.

• *Slow Cooker Size: 5 to 6 qt*

I tbsp	curry powder	15 mL
I tsp	dried thyme leaves	5 mL
I tsp	dried marjoram leaves	5 mL
4	pork loin rib end chops or shoulder butt chops, I inch (2.5 cm) thick, trimmed of excess fat	4
I tbsp	vegetable oil	15 mL
I	large onion, thinly sliced	I
3	cloves garlic, minced	3
I	apple, peeled and chopped	I
½ cup	chicken stock	125 mL
½ cup	dry white wine	125 mL
2 tbsp	honey mustard	25 mL
¼ cup	whipping (35%) cream	50 mL
	Salt and black pepper to taste	

1. In a bowl, combine curry powder, thyme and marjoram. Rub both sides of pork chops with spice mixture.

2. In a large nonstick skillet, heat oil over medium-high heat. Add chops in batches and cook for 5 minutes per side, or until browned. Remove to a plate.

3. Add onion, garlic and apple to drippings in skillet. Cook, stirring, for 2 minutes. Transfer to slow cooker stoneware. Place reserved pork chops over onion mixture. Pour in stock and wine.

4. Cover and cook on **Low** for 4 to 5 hours or on **High** for 2 to 3 hours, or until pork is tender. (Shoulder butt chops should cook on **Low** for 6 to 8 hours or on **High** for 3 to 4 hours.)

5. Remove chops to a platter and cover loosely with foil to keep warm.

6. Stir honey mustard and cream into sauce. Season with salt and pepper. Spoon sauce over pork chops and serve.

Pork Chops with Creamy Mustard Sauce

Makes 4 to 6 servings

This simple dish owes its origins to French country cooking. The creamy mustard sauce goes well with the tender, juicy pork chops.

• *Slow Cooker Size: 3 1/2 to 6 qt*

2	large carrots, peeled and sliced	2
2	parsnips, peeled and sliced	2
1	small shallot, finely chopped	1
2 tbsp	all-purpose flour	25 mL
1 tsp	salt	5 mL
1/2 tsp	black pepper	2 mL
1 tbsp	vegetable oil	15 mL
4 to 6	boneless pork loin rib end chops, 1 inch (2.5 cm) thick, trimmed of excess fat	4 to 6
3/4 cup	dry white wine or undiluted condensed chicken broth	175 mL
1	large onion, sliced	1
1/4 cup	whipping (35%) cream or evaporated milk	50 mL
1 tbsp	Dijon mustard	15 mL

1. Place carrots, parsnips and shallot in slow cooker stoneware. Sprinkle with flour, salt and pepper and toss to coat.

2. In a large nonstick skillet, heat oil over medium-high heat. Add pork chops in batches and cook for 5 minutes per side, or until browned. Remove chops and drain on a paper towel-lined plate to remove any excess oil.

3. Pour wine into skillet and bring to a boil, scraping up any browned bits.

4. Place browned chops on top of vegetables in slow cooker and lay onion slices on top of meat. Pour in wine mixture.

5. Cover and cook on **Low** for 4 to 5 hours or on **High** for 2 to 3 hours, or until meat is tender.

6. With a slotted spoon, remove chops and vegetables from slow cooker and keep warm. Skim fat from juices.

7. In a small bowl, combine cream and mustard. Stir into juices in slow cooker.

8. Cover and cook on **High** for 5 minutes, or until slightly thickened. For a thicker sauce, transfer to a saucepan and bring to a boil. Cook gently for about 5 minutes, or until desired consistency. Serve sauce with pork.

Roasted Potatoes

Scrub 2 lbs (1 kg) potatoes and cut in chunks. Toss with 2 tbsp (25 mL) vegetable or olive oil, $\frac{1}{2}$ tsp (2 mL) salt and $\frac{1}{4}$ tsp (1 mL) black pepper. Place in a greased baking dish and roast in a preheated 425°F (220°C) oven for 50 to 60 minutes, or until tender and golden brown. Turn once during cooking. Makes 4 to 6 servings.

Pork Chops with Spiced Fruit Stuffing

**Makes 4 to
6 servings**

Using storebought
dry stuffing mix makes
this a dish a snap to
prepare. Who would
believe you could eat
something this good
during the week?

You can also use
shoulder butt chops in
this recipe. If so, cook
on **Low** for 6 to 8 hours
or on **High** for 3 to
4 hours, and reduce
the chicken broth by
1/4 cup (50 mL), since
these chops tend to
release more juices
when slow cooked.
This will ensure that
the stuffing does not
become too soggy.

• *Slow Cooker Size: 3 1/2 to 6 qt*

1 tbsp	vegetable oil	15 mL
4 to 6	boneless pork loin rib end chops, 1 inch (2.5 cm) thick, trimmed of excess fat	4 to 6
1/3 cup	raisins	75 mL
1/3 cup	dried cranberries	75 mL
1/3 cup	chopped dried apricots	75 mL
1/4 tsp	salt	1 mL
Pinch	black pepper	Pinch
1/2 cup	apple juice, divided	125 mL
1 cup	chicken stock	250 mL
2 tbsp	butter	25 mL
1/4 tsp	ground cinnamon	1 mL
Pinch	ground nutmeg	Pinch
1	6-oz (175 g) package herb-seasoned stuffing mix	1

1. In a large nonstick skillet, heat oil over medium-high heat. Cook pork chops in batches for about 5 minutes per side, or until browned.

2. Transfer pork to slow cooker stoneware. Sprinkle with raisins, cranberries, apricots, salt, pepper and 1/4 cup (50 mL) apple juice.

3. In a saucepan, combine remaining apple juice, stock, butter, cinnamon and nutmeg. Bring to a boil and stir in dry stuffing and seasoning pouch mix. Remove from heat and spoon over fruit in slow cooker.

4. Cover and cook on **Low** for 4 to 5 hours or on **High** for 2 to 3 hours, or until pork is tender and just a hint of pink remains.

5. To serve, scoop out stuffing and fruit and place in a bowl. Stir gently. Serve with pork chops.

Roast Pork with Two Potatoes

Makes 6 servings

This simple roast is delicately flavored with the licorice accent of fennel, making it an easy but elegant dish for entertaining.

Yellow flesh potatoes such as Yukon Gold look great next to the bright orange color of the sweet potatoes.

• *Slow Cooker Size: 3 1/2 to 6 qt*

2	sweet potatoes, peeled and cut in 1/2-inch (1 cm) cubes	2
2	potatoes, peeled and cut in 1/2-inch (1 cm) cubes	2
2 tsp	fennel seeds	10 mL
1 tsp	dried oregano leaves	5 mL
1 tsp	paprika	5 mL
1/2 tsp	garlic powder	2 mL
1/2 tsp	salt	2 mL
1/4 tsp	black pepper	1 mL
1	boneless pork loin rib end or shoulder butt roast, trimmed of excess fat (about 2 to 3 lbs/1 to 1.5 kg)	1
1 cup	chicken stock	250 mL

1. Place all potatoes in bottom of slow cooker stoneware.

2. With a mortar and pestle or with a rolling pin on a cutting board, crush fennel seeds.

3. In a small bowl, combine crushed fennel seeds, oregano, paprika, garlic powder, salt and pepper. Rub into pork roast. Place seasoned roast on potatoes. Pour stock around meat and vegetables.

4. Cover and cook on **Low** for 10 to 12 hours or on **High** for 5 to 6 hours, or until pork and potatoes are tender.

5. To serve, transfer roast to a cutting board and cover loosely with foil. Let stand for 5 minutes before carving. Slice roast and serve with potatoes.

Pulled Pork Fajitas

**Makes 6 to
8 servings**

Even though this pork
never comes within
spitting distance of a
glowing ember, the flavor
is that of your classic
Carolinian barbecued
pork sandwich.

Leftover pulled
(shredded) pork
can be stored in the
refrigerator for up to
four days or frozen
for up to four months
and used in tacos,
enchiladas and burritos.

You can use a boneless
beef cross rib or rump
roast or 2 lbs (1 kg)
skinless turkey thighs
in place of the pork.

• *Slow Cooker Size: 3½ to 6 qt*

1	boneless pork shoulder butt roast, trimmed of excess fat (about 3 lbs/1.5 kg)	1
1	onion, chopped	1
1 cup	ketchup	250 mL
¾ cup	salsa	175 mL
¾ cup	cola	175 mL
¼ cup	packed brown sugar	50 mL
2 tbsp	rice vinegar	25 mL
4	cloves garlic, minced	4
1 tsp	liquid smoke (page 98)	5 mL
1 tsp	hot red pepper flakes	5 mL
8 to 12	10-inch (25 cm) flour tortillas	8 to 12

1. Place pork in slow cooker stoneware and sprinkle onion over top.

2. In a large bowl, combine ketchup, salsa, cola, brown sugar, vinegar, garlic, liquid smoke and hot pepper flakes. Pour over pork in slow cooker.

3. Cover and cook on **Low** for 10 to 12 hours or on **High** for 5 to 6 hours, or until pork is very tender.

4. Transfer pork to a large bowl and pull meat into shreds using two forks. Skim fat from sauce. Return meat to sauce to keep warm.

5. Wrap tortillas in foil and warm in a preheated 350°F (180°C) oven for 10 minutes. When ready to serve, spoon filling onto warm tortillas and roll up.

Sweet and Sour Pork

**Makes 4 to
6 servings**

Traditional sweet and sour pork is made with deep-fried pork pieces cooked in a sweet-tangy sauce. Ground ginger flavors the sauce in this lean and easy one-pot version.

Serve over cooked rice (page 73) or rice (cellophane) noodles. To prepare them, place noodles in a large bowl of hot water. Soak for about 5 minutes to soften. As soon as noodles are tender, drain in a colander and set aside. Before serving, stir-fry in hot oil for 5 minutes, or until heated through.

• *Slow Cooker Size: 3½ to 6 qt*

1 tbsp	vegetable oil	15 mL
2 lbs	boneless pork shoulder butt roast, trimmed of excess fat, cut in 1-inch (2.5 cm) cubes	1 kg
1 tsp	ground ginger	5 mL
½ tsp	dry mustard	2 mL
1	14-oz (398 mL) can unsweetened pineapple tidbits, with juices	1
3 tbsp	packed brown sugar	45 mL
¼ cup	white vinegar	50 mL
3 tbsp	soy sauce	45 mL
1	red bell pepper, seeded and coarsely chopped	1
3 tbsp	water	45 mL
2 tbsp	cornstarch	25 mL
1 cup	snow peas, cut in half	250 mL

1. In a large nonstick skillet, heat oil over medium-high heat. Add pork in batches and cook, stirring, for 5 to 7 minutes, or until browned on all sides.

2. Return all pork to skillet. Add ginger and mustard and cook, stirring, for 2 minutes.

3. Transfer meat to slow cooker stoneware. Add pineapple, brown sugar, vinegar and soy sauce to slow cooker and stir in.

4. Cover and cook on **Low** for 6 to 8 hours or on **High** for 3 to 4 hours, or until pork is tender.

5. Stir in red pepper. Cover and cook on **High** for 20 minutes.

6. Combine water and cornstarch in a small bowl or jar (page 177). Stir into pork along with snow peas. Cover and cook on **High** for 10 minutes, or until sauce thickens and vegetables are tender-crisp.

Tourtière Shepherd's Pie

Makes 8 servings

This is a perfect dish to turn on before heading out the door to Christmas Eve mass. Serve with a crisp salad of garden greens and chili sauce. (If you make this in a larger slow cooker, the pie will be thinner, but the yield will be the same.)

Make Ahead
This dish can be assembled up to 24 hours before cooking. Cook meat and vegetables and chill separately before assembling in slow cooker. Refrigerate overnight in the slow cooker stoneware. The next day, place stoneware in slow cooker and continue to cook as directed.

• Slow Cooker Size: 3 1/2 to 6 qt

6	potatoes, peeled and cut in 3/4-inch (2 cm) cubes	6
2 lbs	lean ground pork, chicken or turkey	1 kg
1 tbsp	vegetable oil	15 mL
2	onions, finely chopped	2
5	cloves garlic, minced	5
1	stalk celery, finely chopped	1
1 1/2 tsp	dried thyme leaves	7 mL
1/2 tsp	dried savory leaves	2 mL
1/2 tsp	salt	2 mL
1/2 tsp	black pepper	2 mL
1/4 tsp	ground cloves	1 mL
1/4 tsp	ground cinnamon	1 mL
1 cup	chicken stock	250 mL
2 tbsp	chopped fresh parsley	25 mL

1. Cook potatoes in a pot of boiling salted water until tender, about 15 minutes. With a slotted spoon, transfer 1 1/2 cups (375 mL) potatoes to lightly greased slow cooker stoneware. Drain remaining potatoes and return to pot. Mash until smooth.

2. In a large nonstick skillet, cook pork over medium-high heat for 5 to 7 minutes, or until no longer pink. Drain and place in slow cooker.

3. Add oil to pan and heat. Add onions, garlic and celery. Cook, stirring occasionally, for 5 minutes, or until softened.

4. Add thyme, savory, salt, pepper, cloves and cinnamon to skillet. Cook, stirring, for 1 minute, or until fragrant. Add to meat in slow cooker along with stock and parsley. Stir to combine.

5. Spread reserved mashed potatoes over top of meat mixture.

6. Cover and cook on **Low** for 6 to 10 hours or on **High** for 3 to 4 hours, or until bubbling and heated through.

Adobe Pork and Bean Chili

**Makes 6 to
8 servings**

Here's a Southwest
version of pork and
beans. Everyone in
the family will enjoy
this dish, since half
the fun is putting
on all the toppings.
Serve with bowls of
sour cream, crushed
tortilla chips and grated
Cheddar cheese.

• *Slow Cooker Size: 3¹/₂ to 6 qt*

2 tbsp	vegetable oil	25 mL
3 lbs	boneless pork shoulder butt roast, trimmed of excess fat, cut in 1-inch (2.5 cm) cubes	1.5 kg
1	onion, chopped	1
2	cloves garlic, minced	2
2 tbsp	chili powder	25 mL
¹/₂ tsp	cayenne pepper	2 mL
¹/₂ tsp	black pepper	2 mL
1 cup	beef stock	250 mL
1	19-oz (540 mL) can black beans, rinsed and drained, or 2 cups (500 mL) home-cooked beans (page 145)	1
1	19-oz (540 mL) can Italian-style (page 103) stewed tomatoes, with juices	1
1	7¹/₂-oz (213 mL) can tomato sauce	1
1 cup	fresh or frozen and defrosted corn kernels	250 mL

1. In a large nonstick skillet heat 1 tbsp (15 mL) oil
over medium-high heat. Add pork cubes in batches
and cook, stirring, for 5 to 7 minutes, or until pork is
browned on all sides, adding more oil as necessary.
With a slotted spoon, transfer pork to slow cooker
stoneware.

2. Add onion to skillet and cook, stirring, for 3 to 4 minutes,
or until softened.

3. Add garlic, chili powder, cayenne and black pepper
to skillet and cook, stirring, for 1 minute.

4. Add stock to skillet. Bring to a boil, stirring to scrape
up all bits, and pour into slow cooker.

5. Add black beans, tomatoes and tomato sauce to slow
cooker and stir in.

6. Cover and cook on **Low** for 8 to 10 hours or on **High**
for 4 to 5 hours, or until hot and bubbling and pork is
tender.

7. Stir in corn, cover and cook on **High** for 20 to 25
minutes, or until corn is hot.

Italian Meatball
and Bean Ragout

Makes 4 to 6 servings		

This thick, hearty stew is loaded with moist, tender meatballs, vegetables and beans. Serve it with toasted garlic bread.

Look for flavored tomato paste such as roasted garlic or Italian-style. It will add a little more gusto to this dish.

• *Slow Cooker Size: 3 1/2 to 6 qt*

ITALIAN MEATBALLS

1/2 lb	hot or mild Italian sausages, casings removed	250 g
1/2 lb	lean ground pork	250 g
1/2 cup	dry bread crumbs	125 mL
1	small onion, finely chopped	1
3 tbsp	milk	45 mL
1	egg, lightly beaten	1
2 tbsp	grated Parmesan cheese	25 mL
2 tbsp	chopped fresh parsley	25 mL
1/4 tsp	Worcestershire sauce	1 mL
1/4 tsp	salt	1 mL
Pinch	black pepper	Pinch

RAGOUT

1 cup	beef stock	250 mL
1	19-oz (540 mL) can Italian-style (page 103) stewed tomatoes, with juices	1
2 tbsp	tomato paste	25 mL
1	carrot, peeled and chopped	1
1	stalk celery, chopped	1
1	19-oz (540 mL) can white kidney or navy beans, rinsed and drained, or 2 cups (500 mL) home-cooked beans (page 145)	1
1/2 tsp	dried oregano leaves	2 mL
1/2 tsp	salt	2 mL
1/4 tsp	black pepper	1 mL
2 tbsp	grated Parmesan cheese	25 mL

Creamy Spinach Ricotta Noodles (page 137)

Overleaf: Vegetable Chili with Sour Cream Topping (page 148)

Make Ahead
Ragout can be assembled up to 24 hours before cooking. Refrigerate overnight in slow cooker stoneware. The next morning, add meatballs to ragout and place stoneware in slow cooker. Continue to cook as directed. Meatballs can also be cooked up to a month in advance and frozen. Defrost at room temperature for about 30 minutes before adding to ragout.

1. To make meatballs, in a bowl, combine sausage meat, ground pork, bread crumbs, onion, milk, egg, Parmesan, parsley, Worcestershire, salt and pepper. Shape into 1-inch (2.5 cm) balls and place on a foil-lined baking sheet.

2. Bake in a preheated 400°F (200°C) oven for 10 to 12 minutes, or until browned and no longer pink inside.

3. To make ragout, combine stock, tomatoes, tomato paste, carrot, celery, beans, oregano, salt, pepper and cooked meatballs in slow cooker stoneware.

4. Cover and cook on **Low** for 4 to 5 hours, or until sauce is bubbling, meatballs are hot and vegetables are tender.

5. Serve in individual serving bowls and sprinkle with Parmesan cheese.

Toasted Garlic Bread

Cut a loaf of French bread into 1-inch (2.5 cm) slices.

In a bowl, combine ¼ cup (50 mL) softened butter and 3 minced cloves garlic or 1 tsp (5 mL) garlic powder. Spread garlic butter on bread slices.

Place bread on broiler rack butter side up and broil 5 to 6 inches (12 to 15 cm) from heat for 2 to 3 minutes, or until lightly golden brown.

For cheesy garlic bread, sprinkle with ¾ cup (175 mL) grated mozzarella cheese and broil for 3 minutes, or until cheese is melted. Makes 8 to 10 servings.

Oktoberfest
Hot Potato Salad (page 159)

Lamb Shanks with Braised Beans

Makes 4 servings	

In this version of a classic French recipe, economical lamb shanks are cooked slowly in a savory sauce, becoming extremely tender and flavorful. Serve garnished with chopped fresh parsley and accompanied by garlic mashed potatoes to soak up the juices.

• *Slow Cooker Size: 5 to 6 qt*

1 tbsp	vegetable oil	15 mL
4	meaty lamb shanks (2 to 3 lbs/1 to 1.5 kg total)	4
1 tsp	salt	5 mL
½ tsp	black pepper	2 mL
1	19-oz (540 mL) can white beans, rinsed and drained, or 2 cups (500 mL) home-cooked beans (page 145)	1
2	parsnips, peeled and cut in 1-inch (2.5 cm) chunks	2
2	carrots, peeled and cut in 1-inch (2.5 cm) chunks	2
1	onion, quartered	1
½ cup	dry red wine	125 mL
½ cup	chicken stock	125 mL
2 tbsp	tomato paste	25 mL
4	cloves garlic, peeled and halved	4
2 tbsp	finely chopped parsley	25 mL
2 tsp	dried rosemary leaves, crumbled	10 mL
1	bay leaf	1
1 tbsp	chopped fresh parsley	15 mL

1. In a large nonstick skillet, heat oil over medium-high heat. In batches, cook lamb shanks for about 5 to 7 minutes per side, or until brown. Season with salt and pepper.

2. Place beans, parsnips, carrots and onion in slow cooker stoneware. Place meat on top of bean-vegetable mixture.

3. In a bowl, combine wine, stock and tomato paste. Pour over meat and vegetables. Sprinkle with garlic, parsley, rosemary and bay leaf.

4. Cover and cook on **Low** for 8 to 12 hours or on **High** for 4 to 5 hours, or until lamb is very tender and falling off the bones.

5. Using a slotted spoon, transfer meat, beans and vegetables to a platter, cover and keep warm. Discard bay leaf.

6. Skim fat from pan juices and transfer liquid to a saucepan. Boil for 10 minutes to thicken. Spoon juices over meat, beans and vegetables. Garnish with parsley.

Garlic Mashed Potatoes

Peel 2 lbs (1 kg) potatoes and cut into quarters. Place potatoes in a saucepan and cover with water. Add 1 tsp (5 mL) salt. Bring to a boil, cover and reduce heat to medium. Boil gently for 20 to 30 minutes, or until tender. Drain well and return to saucepan.

In a separate small saucepan, heat $\frac{1}{4}$ cup (50 mL) butter over medium heat. Add 2 cloves peeled and crushed garlic and cook for 5 minutes, or until fragrant. Add 1 cup (250 mL) milk, $\frac{1}{2}$ tsp (2 mL) salt and $\frac{1}{2}$ tsp (2 mL) black pepper and heat until milk is hot.

Pour into saucepan with potatoes and mash until smooth. Taste and adjust seasonings if necessary. Makes 4 servings.

Rosemary and Garlic Leg of Lamb

Makes 6 to 8 servings

This recipe takes its inspiration from the Greek isles. The rub-on paste infuses the lamb as it cooks, making the meat fragrant with garlic, lemon and herbs. Slow-roasting this cut ensures juicy, tender results.

Remember to remove the string from the roast before carving and serving.

• *Slow Cooker Size: 6 qt*

6	cloves garlic, peeled and crushed	6
	Grated zest of 1 lemon	
1 tbsp	chopped fresh rosemary, or 1 tsp (5 mL) dried	15 mL
1 tsp	salt	5 mL
½ tsp	black pepper	2 mL
1	3- to 4-lb (1.5 to 2 kg) boneless leg of lamb, tied	1
2 tbsp	olive oil	25 mL
½ cup	dry white wine	125 mL

1. In a small bowl or food processor, mash or chop garlic, lemon zest, rosemary, salt and pepper to form a paste. Rub all over lamb.

2. In a large nonstick skillet, heat oil over medium-high heat. Add lamb and cook, turning meat with tongs or two wooden spoons, for 10 minutes, or until evenly browned on all sides. Transfer meat to slow cooker stoneware.

3. Pour wine into skillet and bring to a boil, scraping to remove any bits from bottom of pan. Pour over meat in slow cooker.

4. Cover and cook on **Low** for 4 to 6 hours, or until meat is tender and cooked to desired doneness.

> ### Checking for Doneness
>
> Use a meat thermometer to test larger cuts of meat for doneness. Roasts continue to cook for 5 to 15 minutes after they are removed from the slow cooker.
> **Rare:** 140°F (60°C)
> **Medium:** 160°F (71°C)
> **Well Done:** 170°F (77°C)

Meatless Main Courses

Banana Walnut French Toast

Makes 8 servings

Serve this make-ahead French toast with maple syrup as a light lunch or brunch dish.

Evaporated milk holds up extremely well in slow cookers and will not curdle. Don't confuse this milk with the sweetened condensed milk used in desserts and candies.

Make Ahead
Assemble ingredients in slow cooker up to 24 hours before cooking.

• *Slow Cooker Size: 5 to 6 qt*

2	ripe bananas, cut in ¼-inch (5 mm) slices	2
2 tbsp	lemon juice	25 mL
1	loaf day-old French bread, crust removed, cut in ½-inch (1 cm) cubes (about 10 cups/2.5 L)	1
3	eggs, lightly beaten	3
1	13-oz (385 mL) can evaporated milk	1
3 tbsp	liquid honey	45 mL
1 tsp	vanilla	5 mL
½ tsp	ground cinnamon	2 mL
1 cup	chopped toasted walnuts (page 151)	250 mL
1 tsp	granulated sugar	5 mL

1. In a bowl, gently toss bananas with lemon juice.

2. Arrange half the bread cubes in bottom of lightly greased slow cooker stoneware. Top bread with bananas. Add remaining bread cubes.

3. In a blender or food processor, combine eggs, evaporated milk, honey, vanilla and cinnamon. Slowly pour egg mixture over bread to coat evenly. Press down lightly with the back of a spoon to moisten all bread.

4. Cover and refrigerate for 8 hours or overnight.

5. Sprinkle bread with walnuts and sugar. Cover and cook on **Low** for 5 to 7 hours or on **High** for 2½ to 3½ hours, or until golden brown and slightly puffed.

Pizza Fondue

**Makes 4 to
6 servings**

This is a wonderful
appetizer dip, but it
also makes a great
weekend family meal
as well as a perfect
potluck dish. Prepare
all the ingredients in
the slow cooker and
cook as directed in
Step 1. Unplug the slow
cooker and wrap in a
towel or newspapers to
insulate, then place in a
container that will stay
flat in the car. Attach
rubber bands around
the handles and lid to
secure when traveling.
Once you arrive, plug in
slow cooker and set on
Low to stay warm.

You can also serve
this with breadsticks,
pretzels and veggies
such as cauliflower
and broccoli.

• *Slow Cooker Size: 3 1/2 to 6 qt*

I	1-lb (500 g) processed cheese loaf, cut in 1/2-inch (1 cm) cubes	I
2 cups	grated mozzarella cheese	500 mL
I	19-oz (540 mL) can Italian-style (page 103) stewed tomatoes, with juices	I
I	loaf Italian bread, cut in 1-inch (2.5 cm) cubes	I

1. Place cheese cubes, mozzarella and tomatoes in lightly greased slow cooker stoneware. Cover and cook on **High** for 45 to 60 minutes, or until cheeses melt.

2. Stir to combine and scrape down sides of slow cooker with a rubber spatula to prevent scorching. Reduce heat to **Low**. (Fondue will stay warm for up to 4 hours.)

3. Serve with bread cubes for dipping.

Corn and Green Chili Tamale Casserole

Makes 4 to 6 servings

I'm always looking for interesting ways to make an easy weeknight meal. Sometimes a few prepared ingredients can be whipped up into a tasty casserole like this one. It's a big hit with my family.

Mexican cuisine includes many raw and cooked salsas based on tomatoes or tomatillos with chilies. Salsa verde is green in color and is found in the Mexican food aisle. If you have difficulty finding it, substitute regular salsa.

Cut the burritos when they are only slightly thawed so the filling doesn't ooze out.

• *Slow Cooker Size: 3 1/2 to 6 qt*

6	prepared bean and cheese burritos, slightly defrosted	6
2 cups	fresh or frozen and defrosted corn kernels	500 mL
1	4 1/2-oz (127 mL) can chopped mild green chilies, including liquid	1
3	green onions, chopped	3
1/4 cup	chopped fresh cilantro, divided	50 mL
1 cup	whipping (35%) cream or sour cream	250 mL
1	7-oz (200 mL) can salsa verde	1
1 tsp	chili powder	5 mL
1/2 tsp	ground cumin	2 mL
1/4 tsp	salt	1 mL
1/4 tsp	black pepper	1 mL
1 1/2 cups	grated Monterey Jack cheese	375 mL
1	avocado, peeled and cut in wedges (optional)	1

1. Cut each burrito into 4 slices and place in a single layer in bottom of slow cooker stoneware. (If you are using a smaller slow cooker, you will have to make two layers of burritos.)

2. Sprinkle burritos with corn, chilies, green onions and 2 tbsp (25 mL) cilantro.

3. In a bowl, whisk together cream, salsa verde, chili powder, cumin, salt and pepper. Pour over burritos and vegetables.

4. Cover and cook on **Low** for 4 to 6 hours or on **High** for 2 to 3 hours, or until heated through and bubbling.

5. Sprinkle casserole with cheese and cook on **High** for 20 to 30 minutes, or until cheese melts. Garnish with remaining cilantro and avocado if using.

Creamy Spinach Ricotta Noodles

Makes 6 to 8 servings

Serve up comfort food to your family with this quick-to-assemble meatless dish.

In Italian, ricotta means recooked, a reference to it being made with leftover whey from milk previously heated for mozzarella and provolone cheese. Ricotta is a fresh white cheese used in both savory and sweet dishes.

• *Slow Cooker Size: 3 1/2 to 6 qt*

2 cups	dried fusilli or other small pasta	500 mL
2 tbsp	butter	25 mL
1	onion, finely chopped	1
1/3 cup	all-purpose flour	75 mL
2 1/2 cups	milk	625 mL
2 tsp	Dijon mustard	10 mL
1 tsp	salt	5 mL
1/2 tsp	black pepper	2 mL
2 cups	ricotta cheese	500 mL
1/2 cup	grated Asiago or Parmesan cheese	125 mL
1	10-oz (300 g) package frozen chopped spinach, defrosted and squeezed dry	1
2	roasted red peppers (page 161), chopped	2
2 tbsp	dry bread crumbs (page 77)	25 mL
2 tbsp	grated Parmesan cheese	25 mL

1. In a large pot of boiling salted water, cook pasta for 7 to 8 minutes, or until almost tender but still firm. Drain.

2. In a large saucepan, melt butter over medium heat. Add onion and cook for 5 minutes, stirring occasionally, until softened. Add flour and cook, stirring, for 1 minute.

3. Whisk in milk and cook, stirring constantly, for 8 to 10 minutes, or until thickened. Stir in mustard, salt and pepper.

4. Add cooked noodles, ricotta, Asiago, spinach and red peppers to sauce. Stir to combine.

5. Transfer mixture to lightly greased slow cooker stoneware and sprinkle with bread crumbs and Parmesan.

6. Cover and cook on **Low** for 6 to 8 hours or on **High** for 3 to 4 hours, or until hot and bubbly.

Slow-cooked Macaroni and Cheese

Makes 8 to 10 servings

Everyone likes good old mac 'n' cheese. While there are many versions, this is one of my quick-and-easy favorites for the slow cooker. The recipe is made even easier with the use of condensed Cheddar cheese soup, which holds up well during the long slow-cooking process.

Use a rolling pin, blender or food processor to crush the melba toast crackers. They will give the casserole a tasty crunch.

Macaroni and Cheese with Ham and Red Pepper
Add 1 cup (250 mL) chopped cooked ham and 1 chopped roasted red pepper (page 161) to macaroni with egg mixture.

• *Slow Cooker Size: 5 to 6 qt*

3 cups	dried elbow macaroni or other small pasta	750 mL
¼ cup	butter, melted	50 mL
2	eggs, lightly beaten	2
1	13-oz (385 mL) can evaporated milk	1
2	10-oz (284 mL) cans condensed Cheddar cheese soup, undiluted	2
1 tsp	dry mustard	5 mL
3 cups	grated Cheddar cheese, divided	750 mL
Pinch	paprika	Pinch
6	melba toast crackers, crushed (optional)	6

1. Cook macaroni in plenty of boiling salted water for 7 to 10 minutes, or until almost tender but still firm. Drain and place in lightly greased slow cooker stoneware. Pour melted butter over macaroni and toss to coat.

2. In a bowl, whisk together eggs, evaporated milk, cheese soup, mustard and 2 cups (500 mL) grated Cheddar. Add to macaroni and stir together.

3. Cover and cook on **Low** for 3 to 4 hours, or until bubbling and edges are lightly browned.

4. In a small bowl, combine remaining Cheddar, paprika and crushed crackers if using. Sprinkle mixture over macaroni.

5. Cover and cook on **Low** for 15 to 20 minutes, or until cheese has melted.

Barbecued Veggie Joes

Makes 8 servings

This is a yummy vegetarian twist on a family favorite. For a Middle Eastern flair, stuff these lentils into pita breads lined with lettuce leaves. The lettuce helps to keep the lentils from soaking the bread.

Lentils are an inexpensive source of protein as well as being high in fiber, complex carbohydrates and B vitamins. It's best to use green or brown lentils in the slow cooker, not the smaller red or yellow lentils, which break down during cooking.

• *Slow Cooker Size: 3 1/2 to 6 qt*

1 cup	dried lentils, rinsed and sorted	250 mL
2 cups	water	500 mL
1 1/2 cups	finely chopped celery	375 mL
1 1/2 cups	finely chopped carrots	375 mL
1	large onion, finely chopped	1
3/4 cup	ketchup	75 mL
2 tbsp	packed brown sugar	25 mL
2 tbsp	Worcestershire sauce	25 mL
2 tbsp	cider vinegar	25 mL
8	kaiser buns, halved and lightly toasted	8
8	slices Cheddar cheese (optional)	8

1. In a saucepan, combine lentils and water. Bring to a boil and reduce heat. Cover and simmer for 10 minutes. Transfer lentils and water to slow cooker stoneware.

2. Add celery, carrots, onion, ketchup, brown sugar and Worcestershire to slow cooker. Mix well.

3. Cover and cook on **Low** for 10 to 12 hours or on **High** for 4 to 6 hours, or until lentils are tender. Just before serving, stir in vinegar.

4. Spoon 1/2 cup (125 mL) filling onto bottoms of toasted kaisers. Top with Cheddar if using and top halves of buns.

Cowpoke Baked Beans

Makes 8 to 10 servings

Cowpokes (just another word for cowboys) called dried beans prairie strawberries, because the varieties they used tended to be reddish-brown in color (i.e., red kidney and pinto). These beans make a great vegetarian main course, but you can also add chopped cooked bacon, or serve them alongside ribs (pages 90, 113, 116 and 117) and coleslaw (page 57).

Make Ahead
This dish can be completely assembled up to 24 hours before cooking. Refrigerate overnight in the slow cooker stoneware. The next day, place stoneware in slow cooker and continue to cook as directed.

• *Slow Cooker Size: 3 1/2 to 6 qt*

2 tbsp	vegetable oil	25 mL
2	onions, chopped	2
4	stalks celery, finely chopped	4
3	cloves garlic, minced	3
2	19-oz (540 mL) cans pinto or Romano beans, rinsed and drained, or 4 cups (1 L) home-cooked beans (page 145)	2
1	19-oz (540 mL) can red kidney beans, rinsed and drained, or 2 cups (500 mL) home-cooked beans	1
1 1/2 cups	salsa	375 mL
1 cup	barbecue sauce	250 mL
1/2 cup	fancy molasses	125 mL
1/4 cup	Dijon mustard	50 mL
1	12-oz (341 mL) bottle beer	1
1/4 cup	chopped fresh parsley	50 mL
	Salt and black pepper to taste	

1. In a large nonstick skillet, heat oil over medium-high heat. Add onions, celery and garlic. Cook, stirring occasionally, for 3 minutes, or until vegetables are softened. With a slotted spoon, transfer onion mixture to slow cooker stoneware.

2. Add beans, salsa, barbecue sauce, molasses, mustard, beer and parsley to slow cooker and stir in.

3. Cover and cook on **Low** for 6 to 10 hours or on **High** for 3 to 4 hours, or until hot and bubbling. Season with salt and pepper.

Cuban-style Black Beans

Makes 6 to 8 servings

Black beans (turtle beans) are a Cuban staple. Top this chili with grated Monterey Jack cheese, chopped tomato and, for an extra kick, a dollop of chipotle-flavored sour cream (combine 1 cup/250 mL sour cream and 1 tsp/5 mL minced chipotles in adobo sauce).

Make Ahead

This dish can be assembled up to 24 hours before cooking. Refrigerate overnight in slow cooker stoneware. The next day, place stoneware in slow cooker and continue to cook as directed.

• *Slow Cooker Size: 3 1/2 to 6 qt*

1	large onion, finely chopped	1
4	cloves garlic, minced	4
3	19-oz (540 mL) cans black beans, rinsed and drained, or 6 cups (1.5 L) home-cooked beans (page 145)	3
1 cup	vegetable stock	250 mL
2 tbsp	granulated sugar	25 mL
2 tbsp	lime juice	25 mL
1/4 tsp	salt	1 mL
1/4 tsp	black pepper	1 mL
1/4 tsp	dried oregano leaves	1 mL
1	bay leaf	1
1	red bell pepper, seeded and finely chopped	1
2 tbsp	finely chopped cilantro	25 mL

1. Combine onion, garlic, beans, stock, sugar, lime juice, salt, pepper, oregano and bay leaf in slow cooker stoneware.

2. Cover and cook on **Low** for 6 to 10 hours or on **High** for 3 to 4 hours, or until hot.

3. Discard bay leaf. Transfer 1 cup (250 mL) hot bean mixture to a bowl and mash slightly with a potato masher. Return to slow cooker.

4. Stir in red pepper and cilantro. Cover and cook on **High** for 15 to 20 minutes, or until heated through.

Chipotle Peppers

Chipotle peppers are smoked jalapeños, but they are considerably hotter than fresh or canned jalapeños. They are available dried or canned in adobo sauce. Look for them in the Mexican food section at the supermarket. Freeze any leftover chipotles in the sauce in ice cube trays and then transfer the small portions to a plastic freezer bag.

Farmer-style Cannellini Beans

**Makes 4 to
6 servings**

This simple combination of white kidney beans (cannellini) seasoned tomatoes and vegetables makes a perfect meatless main course. It also makes a wonderful accompaniment to poultry or meat, and is terrific served cold as a salad. For a non-vegetarian version, garnish with crumbled cooked bacon.

Kale is a dark, leafy green vegetable that is a great source of fiber and many essential nutrients. Remove the stems and any tough veins from the leaves before using.

Make Ahead
This dish can be assembled up to 24 hours before cooking. Refrigerate overnight in slow cooker stoneware. The next day, place stoneware in slow cooker and continue to cook as directed.

• *Slow Cooker Size: 3 1/2 to 6 qt*

1	19-oz (540 mL) can white kidney beans, rinsed and drained, or 2 cups (500 mL) home-cooked beans (page 145)	1
1	19-oz (540 mL) can stewed tomatoes, with juices	1
1/2 cup	vegetable stock	125 mL
1	stalk celery, finely chopped	1
1	onion, finely chopped	1
2	cloves garlic, minced	2
2	bay leaves	2
2 tbsp	olive oil	25 mL
1/2 tsp	dried sage leaves	2 mL
1/2 tsp	dried rosemary leaves, crumbled	2 mL
2 tbsp	dry red wine	25 mL
1 cup	chopped kale leaves	250 mL

1. Combine beans, tomatoes, stock, celery, onion, garlic, bay leaves, olive oil, sage and rosemary in slow cooker stoneware. Stir to combine.

2. Cover and cook on **Low** for 6 to 10 hours or on **High** for 3 to 4 hours, or until hot and bubbling.

3. Stir in wine and kale. Cover and let stand for 5 minutes to wilt kale leaves. Discard bay leaves before serving.

Cilantro

Fresh cilantro, also known as coriander or Chinese parsley, has a distinctive smell and flavor that goes well with many chilies as well as Asian and Indian dishes. To maximize its fairly short refrigerator shelf life, wash the leaves well, spin dry and wrap in a paper towel. Store in a plastic bag in the refrigerator. If the cilantro has roots attached, leave them on; it helps keep the leaves fresh.

Mexican Rice and Beans

This is a wonderful meatless meal the entire family can enjoy. Serve it with a tossed green salad.

Make Ahead
This dish can be assembled and partially prepared up to 24 hours before cooking. Prepare to the end of Step 4 and refrigerate overnight in slow cooker stoneware. The next day, place stoneware in the slow cooker and continue to cook as directed. Cook the rice and prepare the green pepper, cilantro and cheese the night before for an easy dinner preparation when you get home at the end of the day.

• *Slow Cooker Size: 3 1/2 to 6 qt*

1 tbsp	vegetable oil	15 mL
1	onion, finely chopped	1
2	cloves garlic, minced	2
1 tbsp	chili powder	15 mL
1 tsp	ground cumin	5 mL
1/4 tsp	cayenne pepper	1 mL
1/4 tsp	black pepper	1 mL
1	19-oz (540 mL) can tomatoes, chopped, with juices	1
1	19-oz (540 mL) can red kidney beans, rinsed and drained, or 2 cups (500 mL) home-cooked beans (page 145)	1
1 cup	fresh or frozen and defrosted corn kernels	250 mL
2	roasted red peppers (page 161), finely chopped	2
2 cups	cooked rice (about 2/3 cup/150 mL uncooked)	500 mL
1/2	green bell pepper, seeded and chopped	1/2
1 tbsp	chopped fresh cilantro	15 mL
1 cup	grated Cheddar cheese	250 mL

1. In a large nonstick skillet, heat oil over medium-high heat. Add onion and garlic and cook, stirring occasionally, for 5 minutes, or until softened and translucent.

2. Stir in chili powder, cumin, cayenne and pepper and cook, stirring, for 1 minute.

3. Add tomatoes and bring to a boil. Cook, stirring, for 3 minutes, scraping up any bits from bottom of pan.

4. Transfer vegetable mixture to slow cooker stoneware. Stir in kidney beans, corn and roasted red peppers.

5. Cover and cook on **Low** for 6 to 10 hours or on **High** for 3 to 4 hours, or until bubbling.

6. Stir in cooked rice, green pepper and cilantro. Sprinkle top with cheese. Cover and cook on **High** for 15 to 20 minutes, or until heated through and cheese has melted.

Tailgating Four-Bean Hot Dish

Makes 8 to 10 servings

Infamous for brutally cold late-fall temperatures, Green Bay, Wisconsin, is also famous for its football field and tailgating parties. Although fans huddle around grills in boots and parkas, it's still all about the food. A spinoff from traditional baked beans, this hot and hearty combination also goes well with grilled bratwurst or pork chops.

Although you can use canned beans in this recipe, home-cooked dried beans are not only economical, they tend to be better tasting.

For a non-vegetarian version, omit the oil and cook 3 slices chopped bacon with the onion.

• *Slow Cooker Size: 3 1/2 to 6 qt*

1 tbsp	vegetable oil	15 mL
1	large onion, finely chopped	1
1	19-oz (540 mL) can white kidney beans, rinsed and drained, or 2 cups (500 mL) home-cooked beans	1
1	19-oz (540 mL) can red kidney beans, rinsed and drained, or 2 cups (500 mL) home-cooked beans	1
1	19-oz (540 mL) can chickpeas, rinsed and drained, or 2 cups (500 mL) home-cooked chickpeas	1
1	7 1/2-oz (213 mL) can tomato sauce	1
1/2 cup	ketchup	125 mL
2 tbsp	packed brown sugar	25 mL
2 tsp	prepared mustard	10 mL
2 cups	frozen and defrosted green beans	500 mL

1. In a large nonstick skillet, heat oil over medium-high heat. Add onion and cook, stirring occasionally, for 5 minutes, or until tender. Transfer onion to slow cooker stoneware.

2. Add white and red kidney beans, chickpeas, tomato sauce, ketchup, brown sugar and mustard to slow cooker and stir in.

Make Ahead
This dish can be
assembled up to 24
hours before cooking.
Refrigerate overnight in
slow cooker stoneware.
The next day, place
stoneware in slow
cooker and continue
to cook as directed.

3. Cover and cook on **Low** for 6 to 10 hours or on **High** for 3 to 4 hours, or until hot and bubbling.
4. Add green beans to slow cooker. Cover and cook on **High** for 20 to 30 minutes, or until green beans are heated through.

Home-cooked Beans

Remove any dried beans that are broken or cracked, then place beans in a sieve and rinse well under cold running water.

Place beans in a pot and cover with cold water. Bring to a boil on the stove, reduce heat and simmer for 10 minutes. Drain and rinse well.

Transfer beans to slow cooker stoneware and cover with fresh water, about 6 cups (1.5 L) per pound (500 g) beans. Cover and cook on **Low** for 12 to 15 hours, or until tender.

Store cooled beans in the cooking liquid in the refrigerator for up to four days, or drain and freeze in plastic containers until needed.

Perfectly Poached Salmon

Makes 4 to 6 servings

On one of my girls-only outings, I attended a cooking class luncheon. Our instructor, Roger (pronounced the French way), served us a lovely moist poached salmon, and I have adapted the dish to the slow cooker. Serve the salmon hot or cold as part of a buffet, and garnish with slices of lemon and sprigs of parsley and dill.

Make Ahead
Poaching liquid can be made up to 24 hours in advance. Refrigerate until ready to use and reheat on the stove before placing in slow cooker.

• *Slow Cooker Size: 3 1/2 to 6 qt*

POACHING LIQUID

6 cups	water	1.5 L
1 cup	dry white wine	250 mL
2	stalks celery, sliced	2
2	sprigs parsley	2
1	onion, peeled and cut in wedges	1
1	carrot, peeled and sliced	1
1 tsp	dried thyme leaves	5 mL
1/2 tsp	salt	2 mL
1/2 tsp	whole black peppercorns	2 mL
1	bay leaf	1

SALMON

1	salmon fillet (about 3 to 4 lbs/1.5 to 2 kg)	1

CUCUMBER DILL SAUCE

1 cup	mayonnaise	250 mL
1 cup	sour cream	250 mL
1/2 cup	finely chopped cucumber	125 mL
1 tsp	chopped fresh dillweed	5 mL
1/2 tsp	salt	2 mL
1/4 tsp	black pepper	1 mL

1. To prepare poaching liquid, in a saucepan, combine water, wine, celery, parsley, onion, carrot, thyme, salt, peppercorns and bay leaf. Bring to a boil on the stove, reduce heat and simmer for 30 minutes. Strain through a sieve and discard solids. Reserve liquid.

2. To prepare salmon, preheat slow cooker on **High** for 15 minutes. Line slow cooker stoneware with a double thickness of cheesecloth or fold a 2-foot (60 cm) piece of foil in half lengthwise and lay on bottom of slow cooker. Place salmon on top of cheesecloth or foil and pour hot poaching liquid over salmon.

3. Cover and cook on **High** for 1 hour.

4. With oven mitts, remove stoneware from slow cooker and let salmon cool in poaching liquid for 20 minutes. If serving cold, stoneware can be stored in refrigerator to allow salmon to chill in liquid.

5. Lift salmon out of stoneware using cheesecloth or foil handles and gently place on a platter.

6. To prepare sauce, in a bowl, combine mayonnaise, sour cream, cucumber, dill, salt and pepper. Serve salmon with sauce.

Vegetable Chili
with Sour Cream Topping

This vegetarian chili contains lots of fresh vegetables simmered in a rich sauce. The cocoa gives it an authentic Mexican flavor. Serve with cornmeal muffins or breadsticks.

Use a food processor to make quick work of chopping the vegetables. The ground tomatoes give the chili a smooth consistency.

Make Ahead
This chili can be completely assembled up to 24 hours before cooking. Refrigerate overnight in the slow cooker stoneware. The next day, place stoneware in slow cooker and continue to cook as directed. Prepare the sour cream topping and refrigerate until serving.

• *Slow Cooker Size: 3¹/₂ to 6 qt*

1	zucchini, quartered lengthwise and sliced	1
1	stalk celery, chopped	1
1	carrot, peeled and chopped	1
1	onion, finely chopped	1
2	cloves garlic, minced	2
2	14-oz (398 mL) cans kidney beans, drained and rinsed, or 3 cups (750 mL) home-cooked beans (page 145)	2
1	19-oz (540 mL) can tomatoes, chopped, with juices	1
1	14-oz (398 mL) can ground tomatoes	1
¹/₂ cup	vegetable stock	125 mL
1 tbsp	chili powder	15 mL
1 tbsp	unsweetened cocoa powder	15 mL
¹/₂ tsp	dried oregano leaves	2 mL
¹/₂ tsp	ground cumin	2 mL
Dash	hot red pepper sauce	Dash
¹/₂ tsp	salt	2 mL
¹/₄ tsp	black pepper	1 mL
¹/₂ cup	sour cream	125 mL
¹/₂ cup	grated Cheddar cheese	125 mL
4	green onions, chopped	4

1. Combine zucchini, celery, carrot, onion, garlic, kidney beans, tomatoes, ground tomatoes, stock, chili powder, cocoa, oregano, cumin, hot pepper sauce, salt and pepper in slow cooker stoneware.

2. Cover and cook on **Low** for 6 to 8 hours or on **High** for 3 to 4 hours, or until bubbling.

3. In a small bowl, combine sour cream, Cheddar and green onions.

4. Spoon chili into individual serving bowls and add topping.

Grains and
Side Dishes

Good Morning Granola

Makes about 4 cups (1 L)

This crunchy mix is a perfect topping on hot cereal or yogurt. It also tastes great served on its own with milk.

You can replace the cranberry cocktail with an equal amount of frozen apple juice concentrate. Use dried fruit such as cranberries, cherries or chopped apricots.

No-Bake Granola Crunchies

In a double boiler over hot (not boiling) water, melt 1 cup (250 mL) peanut butter, 1 cup (250 mL) milk chocolate chips and ½ cup (125 mL) butter. Stir in 3 cups (750 mL) dry chow mein noodles and 1½ cups (375 mL) granola. Drop by heaping teaspoons onto waxed paper-lined baking sheets. Chill until firm. Store in an airtight container, placing waxed paper between each layer. Refrigerate or freeze for up to two weeks. Makes about 4 dozen cookies.

• Slow Cooker Size: 5 to 6 qt

2 cups	large-flake rolled oats	500 mL
¼ cup	raw wheat germ	50 mL
2 tbsp	sesame seeds	25 mL
½ cup	chopped almonds or pecans	125 mL
½ cup	flaked coconut	125 mL
½ cup	liquid honey	125 mL
¼ cup	frozen cranberry juice cocktail concentrate, defrosted	50 mL
¼ cup	butter, melted	50 mL
2 tbsp	packed brown sugar	25 mL
1½ tsp	vanilla	7 mL
1 cup	dried fruit	250 mL
½ cup	raisins	125 mL

1. Combine oats, wheat germ, sesame seeds, almonds and coconut in slow cooker stoneware.

2. In a bowl, combine honey, cranberry juice concentrate, melted butter, brown sugar and vanilla. Mix well and pour over oat mixture. Stir to combine.

3. Cook, uncovered, on **High** for 2 to 3 hours, or until most of liquid has evaporated. Stir every 30 minutes during cooking time.

4. Reduce heat to **Low**, cover and cook for 3 to 4 hours, or until granola is dry and crisp. Stir frequently to prevent over-browning.

5. Spread granola over a foil-lined baking sheet and cool to room temperature. Mix in dried fruit and raisins and store in an airtight container at room temperature for up to one month.

Maple Pecan Multigrain Porridge

Kick-start your morning with a bowl of this stick-to-your ribs cereal served with milk. Prepare and start cooking the night before, so a bowl of hot porridge is waiting for those early risers.

A sure-fire way to get kids to eat this nutritious cereal is to serve it with a scoop of vanilla ice cream.

Use an uncooked multigrain porridge cereal that contains whole grains such as cracked wheat, rye and flax.

Make Ahead
Assemble ingredients and begin cooking the night before; the porridge will be hot and ready to eat the next morning.

• *Slow Cooker Size: 3 1/2 to 6 qt*

3 cups	water	750 mL
1 cup	uncooked multigrain cereal	250 mL
2 tbsp	maple syrup	25 mL
1/2 tsp	salt	2 mL
1 1/2 tsp	vanilla	7 mL
1/2 cup	chopped toasted pecans or almonds (optional)	125 mL

1. Combine water, cereal, maple syrup, salt and vanilla in slow cooker stoneware.

2. Cover and cook on **Low** for 8 to 10 hours, or until thickened.

3. Spoon into individual serving bowls and sprinkle with chopped nuts if using.

Toasting Nuts

Toasting nuts enhances their flavor and texture. Spread nuts on a baking sheet. Toast at 350°F (160°C) oven for 5 to 7 minutes, or until golden brown, stirring occasionally.

Boston Brown Bread

Makes 3 loaves

This traditional steamed bread is a sweet, harmonious blend of grains and molasses. Serve it warm with any meal.

The bread can be baked in three 19-oz (540 mL) vegetable cans or a 1-lb (500 g) coffee can. An old-fashioned pudding bowl with a lid or a 6-cup (1.5 L) heavy glass mixing bowl will also work well.

• *Slow Cooker Size: 5 to 6 qt*

½ cup	rye flour	125 mL
½ cup	yellow cornmeal	125 mL
½ cup	whole wheat flour	125 mL
3 tbsp	granulated sugar	45 mL
1 tsp	baking soda	5 mL
¾ tsp	salt	4 mL
½ cup	chopped walnuts	125 mL
½ cup	raisins	125 mL
1 cup	buttermilk or sour milk (page 183)	250 mL
⅓ cup	fancy molasses	75 mL

1. In a large bowl, sift together rye flour, cornmeal, whole wheat flour, sugar, baking soda and salt. Stir in walnuts and raisins.

2. In a small bowl, whisk together buttermilk and molasses. Add buttermilk mixture to dry ingredients. Stir until well blended.

3. Spoon mixture evenly into three lightly greased 19-oz (540 mL) cans. Lightly grease three 6-inch (15 cm) pieces of foil. Place a piece of foil, greased side down, on top of each can. Secure foil with elastic bands or string.

4. Place cans in slow cooker stoneware. Add enough boiling water to come halfway up sides of cans. Make sure foil does not touch the water.

5. Cover and cook on **Low** for 3 to 4 hours, or until a tester inserted in center of loaves comes out clean.

6. Remove cans from slow cooker and let cool for 5 minutes. Lay cans on their sides. Roll and tap gently on all sides until bread releases. Remove loaves from cans and cool completely on wire racks.

Johnnycake Cornbread

Makes 8 servings

This is one of my husband's absolute favorites. Serve it as a side dish with chili or stew, or serve thick slices with warm maple syrup for a dessert treat.

You may wish to cook the cornbread with the slow cooker lid slightly ajar to allow any condensation to escape.

In this recipe there is no need to secure the foil with an elastic band or string, since there is no water in the bottom of the slow cooker.

• *Slow Cooker Size: 5 to 6 qt*

1 ¼ cups	all-purpose flour	300 mL
¾ cup	yellow cornmeal	175 mL
¼ cup	granulated sugar	50 mL
1 tsp	baking powder	5 mL
1 tsp	baking soda	5 mL
1 tsp	salt	5 mL
1	egg, lightly beaten	1
1 cup	buttermilk or sour milk (page 183)	250 mL
¼ cup	vegetable oil	50 mL

1. Turn on slow cooker to **Low** to preheat stoneware.

2. In a large bowl, combine flour, cornmeal, sugar, baking powder, baking soda and salt.

3. In a small bowl, whisk together egg, buttermilk and oil.

4. Make a well in center of dry ingredients and pour in liquid ingredients. Mix together just until moistened.

5. Pour batter into a lightly greased 8-cup (2 L) soufflé dish or 2-lb (1 kg) coffee can and cover with foil. Place in bottom of preheated slow cooker stoneware.

6. Cover and cook on **Low** for 3 to 4 hours or on **High** for 1 ½ to 2 hours, or until edges of cornbread are golden and a knife inserted in center comes out clean.

Braised Cabbage and Raspberries

Makes 6 to 8 servings

My mother assisted in the sampling of this dish and described it as "unbelievable." Perfect for the Thanksgiving or Christmas dinner table, it also goes especially well with pork roasts.

Red or green cabbage can be used to make this recipe. The juice from the raspberries will turn the green cabbage bright red and make red cabbage even more vibrant.

* Slow Cooker Size: 3½ to 6 qt

1	medium head green or red cabbage, thinly sliced (about 12 cups/3 L)	1
2	onions, thinly sliced	2
½ cup	dried cranberries	125 mL
2 cups	fresh raspberries, or 1 10-oz (300 g) package frozen unsweetened raspberries, defrosted	500 mL
¾ cup	raspberry vinegar	175 mL
¼ cup	butter, melted	50 mL
½ cup	granulated sugar	125 mL
1 tsp	salt	5 mL

1. Place cabbage, onions, cranberries and raspberries in slow cooker stoneware.

2. In a small bowl, combine vinegar, butter, sugar and salt. Pour over cabbage mixture and toss to combine

3. Cover and cook on **Low** for 4 to 6 hours, or until cabbage is tender.

Scalloped Corn

This is a wonderful summertime side dish.

You can add ½ cup (125 mL) grated Cheddar cheese just before serving. Sprinkle over top of casserole, cover and cook on **High** for 5 minutes, or until melted.

Scalloped Lima Beans

Substitute frozen lima beans for the corn, or you can use a combination of corn and lima beans. Use 2 cups (500 mL) corn kernels and 2 cups (500 mL) frozen lima beans and chop 1 cup (250 mL) of each as directed in the recipe.

• Slow Cooker Size: 3½ to 6 qt

4 cups	fresh or frozen and defrosted corn kernels	1 L
½ tsp	salt	2 mL
½ tsp	dried thyme leaves	2 mL
¼ tsp	black pepper	1 mL
Pinch	ground nutmeg	Pinch
2 tbsp	butter	25 mL
1	onion, finely chopped	1
3 tbsp	all-purpose flour	45 mL
1 cup	milk	250 mL
2 tbsp	grated Parmesan cheese	25 mL

1. In a blender or food processor, coarsely chop 2 cups (500 mL) corn. Place in slow cooker stoneware along with whole corn, salt, thyme, pepper and nutmeg.

2. In a large nonstick skillet, melt butter over medium heat. Add onion and cook, stirring occasionally, for 5 minutes, or until softened. Add flour and cook, stirring, for 1 minute.

3. Add milk, bring mixture to a boil and cook, stirring constantly, for 1 minute, or until thickened. Stir in Parmesan cheese.

4. Stir sauce into corn mixture and combine.

5. Cover and cook on **Low** for 3½ to 4 hours, or until mixture is bubbly around edges.

Honey Lemon Beets

**Makes 6 to
8 servings**

This simple side dish
goes well with any type
of roast. Or use it as
a summer side dish to
accompany barbecued
meats and fish. By
slow cooking the peeled
beets instead of boiling
them, all the beet juices
end up on your plate
instead of going down
the drain.

Make Ahead
This dish can be
completely assembled
up to 24 hours before
cooking. Refrigerate
overnight in the slow
cooker stoneware.
The next day, place
stoneware in slow
cooker and continue
to cook as directed.

• *Slow Cooker Size: 3 1/2 to 6 qt*

1 tbsp	butter	15 mL
1	onion, sliced	1
8	beets, peeled and quartered	8
2 tbsp	liquid honey	25 mL
2 tbsp	lemon juice	25 mL
1/2 tsp	ground nutmeg	2 mL
1/4 tsp	salt	1 mL
1/4 tsp	black pepper	1 mL
1/2 cup	vegetable stock	125 mL

1. In a skillet over medium heat, melt butter. Add onion
   and cook, stirring occasionally, for about 5 minutes,
   or until softened.

2. Place beets in slow cooker stoneware. Add cooked
   onion, honey, lemon juice, nutmeg, salt, pepper and
   stock. Stir to combine.

3. Cover and cook on **Low** for 8 to 10 hours or on **High**
   for 4 to 5 hours, or until beets are tender.

Leeks

Leeks have a wonderful mellow flavor when they
are cooked gently before being added to sauces
or other dishes. They must be cleaned carefully
before using, since they tend to contain a lot of
sand. Remove the roots and dark-green tops.
Cut the leek in half lengthwise. Rinse thoroughly
under cold running water and drain in a colander.

Scalloped Sweet Potatoes and Parsnips

Makes 6 to 8 servings

This delectable side dish almost outshines the turkey or ham. And there's less to fuss about when there's company and you have a standby vegetable cooking in the slow cooker. It frees up the oven for other dishes.

Parsnips are a sweet root vegetable; they look like white carrots. If you have a hard time finding them, substitute carrots.

Make Ahead

This dish can be completely assembled up to 24 hours before cooking. Refrigerate overnight in slow cooker stoneware. The next day, place stoneware in slow cooker and continue to cook as directed.

• *Slow Cooker Size: 3½ to 6 qt*

3 tbsp	butter	45 mL
2	leeks, white and light-green parts only, rinsed and thinly sliced	2
3 tbsp	all-purpose flour	45 mL
1½ cups	whipping (35%) cream	375 mL
1 tsp	salt	5 mL
1 tsp	dry mustard	5 mL
½ tsp	dried thyme leaves	2 mL
¼ tsp	black pepper	1 mL
2	sweet potatoes, peeled and cut in ¼-inch (5 mm) slices	2
2	parsnips, peeled and cut in ¼-inch (5 mm) slices	2
2 tbsp	grated Parmesan cheese	25 mL

1. In a large nonstick skillet, melt butter over medium-low heat. Add leeks and cook, stirring, for 8 to 10 minutes, or until softened. Add flour and cook, stirring constantly, for 1 minute.

2. Slowly whisk in cream, salt, mustard, thyme and pepper. Increase heat to medium-high and bring to a boil. Reduce heat and cook, stirring, for about 5 minutes, or until smooth and slightly thickened.

3. Layer sweet potatoes and parsnips in lightly greased slow cooker stoneware. Pour cream sauce over top. Sprinkle with Parmesan cheese.

4. Cover and cook on **Low** for 5 to 7 hours or on **High** for 3 to 4 hours, or until sweet potatoes are tender.

Maple Pecan Squash Wedges

**Makes 8 to
10 servings**

This divine side dish
is destined to become
a Thanksgiving
dinner classic.

If you can't find
butternut squash, use
another winter squash
such as Hubbard or
buttercup.

Make Ahead

This dish can be
completely assembled
up to 24 hours before
cooking. Refrigerate
overnight in the slow
cooker stoneware.
The next day, place
stoneware in the slow
cooker and continue
to cook as directed.

• *Slow Cooker Size: 3 1/2 to 6 qt*

1	butternut squash, about 3 lbs (1.5 kg)	1
1/4 cup	maple syrup	50 mL
2 tbsp	butter, melted	25 mL
1 tsp	grated orange zest	5 mL
1/2 tsp	grated gingerroot	2 mL
1/2 tsp	salt	2 mL
1/2 tsp	black pepper	2 mL
1/4 cup	chopped pecans, toasted (page 151)	50 mL

1. Wash squash and cut in half lengthwise, leaving outside skin on. Remove seeds and cut each half horizontally into slices 1 inch (2.5 cm) thick. Lay slices in bottom of slow cooker stoneware.

2. In a bowl, combine maple syrup, melted butter, orange zest, gingerroot, salt and pepper. Pour over squash slices.

3. Cover and cook on **Low** for 6 to 8 hours or on **High** for 3 to 4 hours, or until slices are fork-tender. Sprinkle with pecans before serving.

Winter Squash

Once the fall harvest season rolls around, there
are many winter squash varieties to choose from.
Look for types with bright orange flesh, such as
Hubbard, butternut or buttercup. If you are not a
squash fan, sweet potatoes are a good alternative.
Some supermarkets sell fresh pre-chopped
squash, which saves you the trouble of peeling.

Oktoberfest Hot Potato Salad

Makes 6 servings

Oktoberfest is an annual event in my community, and you can't visit a single festhall without being tempted by a sausage on a bun and a helping of this delicious potato dish.

The beer gives this salad a wonderful rich flavor, but if you prefer, you can substitute water.

• *Slow Cooker Size: 3½ to 6 qt*

5	potatoes, peeled, quartered and cut in 1-inch (2.5 cm) chunks (about 2½ lbs/1.25 kg)	5
1	large onion, finely chopped	1
2	stalks celery, finely chopped	2
2 tbsp	all-purpose flour	25 mL
2 tbsp	granulated sugar	25 mL
1 tsp	salt	5 mL
½ tsp	celery seed	2 mL
¼ tsp	black pepper	1 mL
½ cup	dark beer or water	125 mL
⅓ cup	cider vinegar	75 mL
4	slices bacon, cooked crisp and crumbled	4
2 tbsp	chopped fresh parsley	25 mL

1. Place potatoes, onion and celery in slow cooker stoneware.

2. In a small bowl, combine flour, sugar, salt, celery seed and pepper. Mix well and sprinkle over vegetables in slow cooker. Toss to coat.

3. Pour beer and vinegar over potatoes.

4. Cover and cook on **High** for 6 to 8 hours, or until potatoes are tender.

5. Stir in bacon. Spoon potato salad into serving bowl and sprinkle with parsley.

Veggie-stuffed Baked Potatoes

Makes 6 servings

No one will believe you made these in the slow cooker. They make a satisfying vegetarian main course, or you can serve them as a side dish with grilled chicken or steak.

If you are pressed for time, omit the mashing step and just serve the baked potatoes with a variety of toppings, including sour cream, ranch dip, bacon bits, crumbled blue cheese and salsa. Or serve with hot baked beans or leftover spaghetti sauce and grated mozzarella cheese.

Tossing the potatoes with oil before cooking helps keep the skins soft. Salt and pepper the skins, too, for those who like to eat the whole potato, skins and all!

- Slow Cooker Size: $3^{1}/_{2}$ to 6 qt

6	large baking potatoes, unpeeled (about 3 lbs/1.5 kg total)	6
2 tbsp	vegetable oil	25 mL
$1^{1}/_{2}$ tsp	salt, divided	7 mL
$^{3}/_{4}$ tsp	black pepper, divided	3 mL
2 tbsp	butter	25 mL
$^{1}/_{2}$ cup	milk	125 mL
$^{1}/_{2}$ cup	sour cream	125 mL
1 tsp	Dijon mustard	5 mL
$^{1}/_{2}$ tsp	salt	2 mL
$^{1}/_{4}$ tsp	black pepper	1 mL
1 cup	small broccoli florets	250 mL
1	carrot, peeled and shredded or finely chopped	1
$^{1}/_{2}$ cup	chopped red bell pepper	125 mL
$^{1}/_{2}$ cup	grated Cheddar cheese	125 mL

1. Pierce potatoes all over with a fork. Rub potato skins with oil and sprinkle with 1 tsp (5 mL) salt and $^{1}/_{2}$ tsp (2 mL) pepper. Wrap potatoes individually in foil and place in slow cooker stoneware.

2. Cover and cook on **Low** for 6 to 10 hours, or until potatoes are tender.

3. Remove potatoes from slow cooker and unwrap. Slice $^{1}/_{4}$ inch (5 mm) off each potato. Scoop potato flesh into a bowl, leaving skins intact.

4. Add butter, milk, sour cream, mustard and remaining salt and pepper to potato flesh and mash until smooth and blended. Stir in broccoli, carrot, red pepper and cheese. Spoon mashed potato mixture back into skins.

5. Place potatoes on a baking sheet and bake in a preheated 400°F (200°C) oven for 15 to 20 minutes, or until tops are golden.

Double Berry Maple Crumble (page 174)

Lisa's Classic Green Beans

Makes 4 to 6 servings

My friend Lisa Wilson (who claims she is not much of a cook, though she is a good lawyer) always brings the best vegetable side dishes to our potluck dinners. While the original recipe contained canned green beans, Lisa updated it by using frozen French-cut beans. A can of condensed mushroom soup is used because it stands up well during the long cooking time.

If you can't find French-cut frozen green beans, regular-cut frozen beans can be substituted (fresh beans tend not to work as well in this recipe).

Double Chocolate Caramel Bread Pudding (page 176)

• *Slow Cooker Size: 3 1/2 to 6 qt*

1	10-oz (284 mL) can condensed cream of mushroom soup, undiluted	1
2 tbsp	sour cream	25 mL
1/2 tsp	salt	2 mL
1/2 tsp	black pepper	2 mL
1 tbsp	chopped fresh parsley	15 mL
1 tsp	dried sage leaves	5 mL
1/4 tsp	ground nutmeg	1 mL
4 cups	frozen French-cut green beans, defrosted	1 L
1	onion, finely chopped	1
1/2 cup	finely chopped roasted red pepper (page 161)	125 mL
1/2 cup	slivered or sliced almonds, toasted (page 151)	125 mL

1. In a bowl, whisk together soup, sour cream, salt, pepper, parsley, sage and nutmeg. Add frozen beans, onion and roasted red pepper. Toss to coat in soup mixture. Transfer to slow cooker stoneware.

2. Cover and cook on **Low** for 3 to 4 hours, or until hot and bubbling. Spoon into serving dish and sprinkle with toasted almonds.

Roasting Peppers

For convenience, roasted red peppers are available in jars or can be found fresh in the deli section of some supermarkets. To make your own, preheat broiler and cut peppers in half, removing ribs and seeds. Place cut side down on a baking sheet. Place peppers about 6 inches (15 cm) from broiler element and broil until skins turn black. Place peppers in a paper bag. Close bag and allow peppers to sweat for about 30 minutes. Peel off skins and chop as needed.

Barley Mushroom "Risotto"

Makes 6 servings

I adore risotto and would eat it every day if I had the chance. This slow cooker version uses barley to produce a dish very similar to the real thing. Although this makes a hearty meatless main course, it can also be served as a side dish with beef, pork, chicken or lamb.

Pearl barley, which is the common form of barley, is the perfect grain to cook in the slow cooker. The long, slow cooking makes it tender but not gummy.

Shrimp Mushroom Risotto

Stir in ½ lb (250 g) peeled, deveined and cooked shrimp during the final 10 minutes of cooking time.

• *Slow Cooker Size: 3½ to 6 qt*

1	½-oz (14 g) package dried wild mushrooms, such as shiitake or chanterelles	1
1 cup	boiling water	250 mL
1 cup	uncooked pearl barley	250 mL
1	onion, finely chopped	1
½ tsp	salt	2 mL
¼ tsp	black pepper	1 mL
2 cups	vegetable stock	500 mL
¼ cup	dry white wine	50 mL
½ cup	grated Parmesan cheese	125 mL
¼ cup	pine nuts, toasted	50 mL

1. Place mushrooms in a small bowl and pour boiling water over top. Allow to stand for 15 minutes, or until softened. Strain, reserving liquid. Finely chop mushrooms.

2. Combine barley, onion, salt, pepper, stock, wine, chopped mushrooms and reserved mushroom liquid in slow cooker stoneware.

3. Cover and cook on **Low** for 4 to 6 hours, or until barley is tender and liquid has been absorbed.

4. Just before serving, stir in Parmesan cheese and pine nuts.

Pine Nuts

Pine nuts are the sweet edible seeds of pine trees that grow in the southwest United States and Mexico. To toast them, spread on a baking sheet and toast in a 350°F (160°C) oven for about 10 minutes, or until golden brown.

Middle Eastern Pilaf

Makes 4 to 6 servings

Fragrant with cinnamon and spices and filled with colorful vegetables, this may be one of the best vegetarian dishes I have ever tasted.

Lentils come in a variety of colors. Try to use green or brown lentils in this dish; the smaller red lentils will break down during cooking.

When preparing the ingredients, be sure to grate the orange zest before you squeeze out the juice.

Make Ahead

Cook rice and toast almonds the day before so you can quickly stir them into the finished dish. The rest of the dish can be assembled up to 24 hours before cooking. Refrigerate overnight in slow cooker stoneware. The next day, place stoneware in slow cooker and continue to cook as directed.

• *Slow Cooker Size: 3 1/2 to 6 qt*

1 tbsp	butter	15 mL
1	onion, finely chopped	1
2	cloves garlic, minced	2
1/4 tsp	hot red pepper flakes	1 mL
1/4 tsp	ground cinnamon	1 mL
1/4 tsp	ground coriander	1 mL
Pinch	ground allspice or cloves	Pinch
1	19-oz (540 mL) can brown lentils, rinsed and drained, or 2 cups (500 mL) home-cooked lentils	1
2	carrots, peeled and shredded or finely chopped	2
1/2 cup	vegetable stock or water	125 mL
1/2 cup	orange juice	125 mL
1/2 tsp	salt	2 mL
2 cups	cooked rice (about 2/3 cup/150 mL uncooked)	500 mL
2 cups	baby spinach leaves, trimmed	500 mL
1/2 tsp	grated orange zest	2 mL
1 tbsp	lemon juice	15 mL
1/4 cup	slivered almonds, toasted (page 151)	50 mL
1/4 cup	currants (optional)	50 mL

1. In a large nonstick skillet, heat butter over medium-high heat. Add onion and garlic and cook, stirring occasionally, for 5 minutes, or until softened.

2. Add hot pepper flakes, cinnamon, coriander and allspice to skillet. Cook, stirring, for 1 minute, or until fragrant.

3. Transfer onion mixture to slow cooker stoneware. Add lentils, carrots, stock, orange juice and salt. Stir to combine.

4. Cover and cook on **Low** for 6 to 8 hours or on **High** for 3 to 4 hours, or until hot and bubbling.

5. Add rice, spinach, orange zest, lemon juice, almonds and currants if using. Stir to combine.

6. Cover and cook on **High** for 10 to 15 minutes, or until heated through and spinach has wilted.

Country-style Sage and Bread Stuffing

Makes 10 to 12 servings

Is it stuffing or dressing? Technically, it's stuffing when it's baked inside the bird and dressing when it's not. Whichever the case, stuffing cooked inside the slow cooker is moist, delicious and a lot easier to get out!

Dried Fruit Stuffing

Add 1 cup (250 mL) chopped dried fruit such as cranberries, apples, raisins and currants to stuffing and stir in for last hour of cooking.

Mushroom Stuffing

In a large skillet, melt 1/4 cup (50 mL) butter over medium heat. Add 1 1/2 lbs (750 g) sliced mushrooms and cook, stirring often, for 10 to 12 minutes, or until liquid has evaporated and mushrooms are beginning to brown. Stir cooked mushrooms into stuffing for last hour of cooking.

• *Slow Cooker Size: 3 1/2 to 6 qt*

1/2 cup	butter	125 mL
2	onions, finely chopped	2
2	stalks celery, finely chopped	2
1/2 cup	finely chopped fresh parsley	125 mL
1 1/2 tsp	dried rosemary leaves, crumbled	7 mL
1 1/2 tsp	dried thyme leaves	7 mL
1 1/2 tsp	dried marjoram leaves	7 mL
1 1/2 tsp	dried sage leaves	7 mL
1 1/2 tsp	salt	7 mL
1/2 tsp	ground nutmeg	2 mL
1/2 tsp	black pepper	2 mL
1	loaf day-old sourdough bread, cut in 1/2-inch (1 cm) cubes (about 10 cups/2.5 L)	1
1 1/2 cups	chicken, turkey or vegetable stock	375 mL

1. In a large nonstick skillet, heat butter over medium-high heat. Add onions and celery and cook, stirring occasionally, for about 10 minutes, or until onions are softened.

2. Add parsley, rosemary, thyme, marjoram, sage, salt, nutmeg and pepper. Cook, stirring, for 1 minute.

3. Place bread cubes in a large bowl and add onion mixture. Toss gently to combine. Slowly add stock, tossing gently to moisten. Transfer to slow cooker stoneware.

4. Cover and cook on **High** for 1 hour. Reduce heat to **Low** and continue to cook for 2 to 3 hours, or until heated through. (The slow cooker will keep the stuffing at serving temperature. Keep on **Low** for up to 3 hours after stuffing is cooked.)

Wild Rice Stuffing with Almonds and Cranberries

Makes 8 to 10 servings

This is a delicious special-occasion accompaniment to any roast, especially roast pork.

Wild rice is not actually rice but a long-grain marsh grass native to the northern Great Lakes region. It has a wonderful nutty flavor and chewy texture that enhance stuffings, casseroles, soups and salads.

• *Slow Cooker Size: 3 1/2 to 6 qt*

1/2 cup	butter	125 mL
1	large onion, finely chopped	1
2	cloves garlic, minced	2
1/4 cup	chopped fresh parsley	50 mL
1 tbsp	chopped fresh thyme, or 1 tsp (5 mL) dried	15 mL
3 cups	chicken or vegetable stock	750 mL
1 cup	uncooked wild rice	250 mL
1 cup	cooked rice (about 1/4 cup/50 mL uncooked)	250 mL
1/2 cup	dried cranberries	125 mL
1/2 cup	chopped almonds, (page 151)	125 mL
1/2 cup	chopped green onions	125 mL
	Salt and black pepper to taste	

1. In a large nonstick skillet, melt butter over medium-high heat. Add onion and garlic and cook, stirring occasionally, for 4 to 5 minutes, or until softened.

2. Add parsley and thyme. Cook, stirring, for 1 minute.

3. Transfer onion mixture to slow cooker stoneware. Stir in stock and wild rice.

4. Cover and cook on **Low** for 6 to 8 hours or on **High** for 3 to 4 hours, or until most of liquid has been absorbed and rice fluffs easily with a fork.

5. Add cooked rice, cranberries, almonds and green onions to slow cooker. Stir to combine. Cover and cook on **High** for 20 to 30 minutes, or until heated through. Season with salt and pepper.

Rhubarb Apple Sauce

Makes about 2¹⁄₂ cups (625 mL)

A sure sign of spring is the popping up of tender pink rhubarb shoots. Make this tangy-sweet sauce to serve over grilled chicken or pork or alongside a roast.

The sauce will keep in the refrigerator for up to one week or in the freezer for up to three months.

- Slow Cooker Size: 3¹⁄₂ to 4 qt

2 cups	chopped fresh or frozen and defrosted rhubarb	500 mL
1 cup	unsweetened applesauce	250 mL
2 tbsp	cider vinegar	25 mL
¹⁄₄ cup	packed brown sugar	50 mL
¹⁄₄ cup	granulated sugar	50 mL
¹⁄₂ tsp	ground cinnamon	2 mL

1. Combine rhubarb, applesauce, vinegar, brown sugar, granulated sugar and cinnamon in slow cooker stoneware.

2. Cover and cook on **Low** for 3 to 4 hours or **High** for 1 to 2 hours, or until tender.

Sweet Endings

Amaretti Pear Crisp

This is a wonderful dessert to serve in pear season. Amaretti cookies are available at most Italian delis and supermarkets. Gingersnaps are a good alternative, or you can use honey Graham crackers, though they will give this dish a very different taste.

Serve the crisp warm with vanilla ice cream, Devon-style custard or whipped cream.

• *Slow Cooker Size: 3 ½ to 6 qt*

3 lbs	ripe pears (about 7 or 8)	1.5 kg
½ cup	chopped dried apricots	125 mL
¼ cup	granulated sugar	50 mL
¼ cup	Amaretto liqueur, dark rum or pear nectar	50 mL

TOPPING

1 cup	crushed Amaretti or gingersnap cookies (page 95)	250 mL
½ cup	all-purpose flour	125 mL
⅓ cup	packed brown sugar	75 mL
2 tbsp	granulated sugar	25 mL
⅓ cup	cold butter, cut in cubes	75 mL

1. Peel pears, cut in half, remove cores and cut each half into 3 slices.

2. In a large bowl, combine pears, apricots, granulated sugar and Amaretto. Transfer to slow cooker stoneware.

3. To prepare topping, in a separate bowl, combine cookie crumbs, flour, brown sugar and granulated sugar.

4. With a pastry blender or two knives, cut in butter until mixture resembles small peas. Sprinkle over pear mixture.

5. Cover and cook on **Low** for 6 to 8 hours or on **High** for 3 to 4 hours, or until tender.

Bananas with Honey-roasted Nuts

Serve this with vanilla ice cream and drizzle a little banana liqueur (or your favorite liqueur) on top before serving.

Look for bananas with skins that still show a little green. They will be slightly firm to start but will soften as they cook. To stop the bananas from turning brown too quickly, rub or brush the cut sides with a little lemon juice after peeling.

Buy honey-roasted peanuts or make your own (page 30).

• *Slow Cooker Size 3 1/2 to 6 qt*

1 cup	packed brown sugar	250 mL
1/3 cup	butter, melted	75 mL
1 tbsp	hot water	15 mL
1/2 tsp	vanilla	2 mL
8	bananas, just ripened, peeled and halved lengthwise	8
1/2 cup	chopped honey-roasted peanuts	125 mL

1. In a small bowl, combine brown sugar, melted butter, water and vanilla. Mix well.

2. Arrange bananas, cut side up, in bottom of lightly greased slow cooker stoneware. Pour sugar mixture over bananas.

3. Cover and cook on **Low** for 3 to 4 hours, or until sauce is bubbling.

4. Spoon warm bananas into serving bowls and sprinkle with chopped peanuts.

Apricot Croissant Pudding with Caramel Sauce

Makes 10 to 12 servings

Croissants and orange liqueur make this bread pudding super decadent. If you are short of time, use a storebought caramel sauce.

You'll need about twelve large croissants, or buy twice as many mini croissants, which chop up nicely. Many supermarkets now carry the frozen variety, which need to be baked first.

Make Ahead
The caramel sauce can be prepared a day ahead. Cover and chill. Rewarm in a saucepan over medium-low heat before serving.

• *Slow Cooker Size: 5 to 6 qt*

3	13-oz (385 mL) cans evaporated milk	3
6	eggs, lightly beaten	6
1/2 cup	granulated sugar	125 mL
1/4 cup	Grand Marnier or orange juice	50 mL
1/2 tsp	ground nutmeg	2 mL
12 cups	chopped croissants	3 L
1 cup	chopped dried apricots	250 mL

CARAMEL SAUCE

1 cup	granulated sugar	250 mL
2 tbsp	water	25 mL
2 tbsp	corn syrup	25 mL
1/2 cup	whipping (35%) cream	125 mL
1/4 cup	butter	50 mL
1/2 tsp	vanilla	2 mL

1. To make pudding, in a large bowl, whisk together evaporated milk, eggs, sugar, Grand Marnier and nutmeg until smooth.

2. Place croissant pieces in lightly greased slow cooker stoneware. Add apricots and toss to combine.

3. Pour custard over croissant-apricot mixture, pressing down gently with a spatula so croissants and apricots are evenly covered. Let stand for 20 minutes.

4. Cover and cook on **High** for 3 to 4 hours, or until pudding is golden brown on top and firm to touch. (If sides begin to burn, reduce heat to **Low** and continue as directed.) Cool slightly.

5. Meanwhile, to prepare sauce, in a saucepan, combine sugar, water and corn syrup over medium-low heat until sugar dissolves. Increase heat to medium-high. Boil without stirring for about 8 minutes, or until syrup turns amber. Brush down sides of pan with a wet pastry brush and swirl pan occasionally.

6. Remove sauce from heat. Whisk in whipping cream, butter and vanilla (mixture will bubble vigorously).

7. Place pan over low heat and cook, stirring, for about 2 minutes, or until sauce thickens slightly.

8. Spoon pudding into individual bowls and drizzle with caramel sauce.

Basic-but-Beautiful Slow Cooker Cheesecake

You won't believe how perfectly a cheesecake turns out when you cook it in the slow cooker — smooth and creamy, without a single crack. Make sure your pan will fit in the slow cooker before you begin to make this recipe.

If you are short of time, serve this with a storebought fruit topping or fresh berries.

Make Ahead
This cake is best made a day ahead and allowed to chill in the refrigerator overnight. You can also freeze the cake for up to two weeks.

• *Slow Cooker Size: 5 to 7 qt*

CRUST
¾ cup	vanilla wafer crumbs (about 15 wafers)	175 mL
2 tbsp	granulated sugar	25 mL
3 tbsp	butter, melted	45 mL

CHEESECAKE
2	8-oz (250 g) packages cream cheese, softened	2
½ cup	granulated sugar	125 mL
¼ cup	sour cream	50 mL
2	eggs, lightly beaten	2
1 tsp	vanilla	5 mL

FRUIT TOPPING
1	10-oz (300 g) package frozen raspberries, strawberries or blueberries, defrosted	1
⅓ cup	granulated sugar	75 mL
2 tbsp	cornstarch	25 mL
1 tbsp	lemon juice	15 mL

1. To prepare crust, in a bowl, combine wafer crumbs, sugar and melted butter. Mix well and press into a well-greased 7- or 8-inch (17 or 20 cm) springform pan. Freeze until ready to use.

2. To prepare cheesecake, in a large bowl or food processor, combine cream cheese, sugar and sour cream. Process or beat with an electric mixer until smooth.

3. Beat in eggs one at a time, mixing well after each addition. Beat in vanilla.

Mocha Marble Cheesecake

Substitute chocolate wafer crumbs for vanilla wafers and omit sugar in crust. After preparing batter, set aside 1 cup (250 mL) batter mixture. Dissolve 2 tsp (10 mL) instant coffee granules in 1 tbsp (15 mL) hot water. Fold 6 oz (175 g) melted and cooled semisweet chocolate into remaining batter along with coffee. Spread all but ½ cup (125 mL) chocolate batter in prepared pan. Spread plain mixture evenly on top. Top with remaining chocolate mixture and swirl with a knife to marble. Bake as directed.

4. Pour cheesecake mixture into prepared crust. Wrap entire pan tightly with foil and secure foil with an elastic band or string.

5. Place pan in slow cooker stoneware lined with cheesecloth or foil strips (page 14). Pour in enough boiling water to come 1 inch (2.5 cm) up sides of springform. (If your pan fits snugly in slow cooker, add water before inserting pan.)

6. Cover and cook on **High** for 3 to 4 hours, or until edges are set and center is just slightly jiggly. Remove from slow cooker and chill thoroughly, preferably overnight, before serving.

7. Meanwhile, to make fruit topping, drain berries and reserve juice.

8. In a small saucepan, combine sugar and cornstarch. Stir in lemon juice and reserved berry juice. Bring to a boil over medium heat and simmer, stirring, for 1 minute. Remove from heat and stir in defrosted fruit. Chill.

9. Just before serving, spread topping over cheesecake.

Double Berry Maple Crumble

Makes 6 servings

Blueberries and blackberries are a wonderful combination in this old-fashioned crumble. If you can't find blackberries, substitute raspberries.

Fruit crisps and crumbles have a natural affinity for cream, whether it's ice cream, sour cream, or whipped cream, but you can cut back on the fat by serving this with frozen vanilla yogurt, light sour cream or fresh fruit yogurt instead.

If you are using frozen berries, there is no need to defrost them. As the slow cooker heats up, it will thaw and cook the fruit.

• *Slow Cooker Size: 3 1/2 to 6 qt*

1 cup	all-purpose flour	250 mL
1/2 cup	chopped walnuts	125 mL
2/3 cup	packed brown sugar	150 mL
1/2 cup	cold butter, cut in cubes	125 mL
4 cups	fresh or frozen blueberries	1 L
1 cup	fresh or frozen blackberries or raspberries	250 mL
2/3 cup	maple syrup	150 mL
1 tbsp	cornstarch	15 mL
2 tbsp	lemon juice	25 mL

1. In a bowl, combine flour, walnuts and brown sugar. Cut in butter using a pastry blender or two knives until well blended and mixture is the size of small peas.

2. Combine blueberries, blackberries, maple syrup, cornstarch and lemon juice in slow cooker stoneware. Toss to coat. Sprinkle topping over berries.

3. Cover and cook on **Low** for 6 to 8 hours or on **High** for 3 to 4 hours, or until fruit is tender and juices bubble.

Brown Sugar and Coconut Baked Apples

Makes 6 servings

Come home to the wonderful smell of apples baking with butter and spices. If you wish, sprinkle the baked apples with a little toasted coconut (page 61) before serving.

If you have an odd apple that doesn't want to stand upright in the slow cooker, cut a thin slice off the bottom.

This dish is best made in a large oval slow cooker. If you have a smaller model, reduce the apples to 3 or 4 (depending on what you can fit in) and make half the filling mixture.

• *Slow Cooker Size: 5 to 6 qt*

6	baking apples, such as Cortland, Spy or McIntosh	6
2 tbsp	packed brown sugar	25 mL
2 tbsp	flaked coconut	25 mL
I tsp	ground cinnamon	5 mL
½ tsp	ground nutmeg	2 mL
3 tbsp	maple syrup	45 mL
6 tbsp	cold butter	75 mL
I cup	apple juice	250 mL

1. Peel skin off top quarter of each apple. Using a melon baller, scoop out core, leaving bottom of apple intact. Stand apples upright in slow cooker stoneware.

2. In a bowl, combine brown sugar, coconut, cinnamon and nutmeg. Fill apple cavities with sugar mixture.

3. Spoon about 2 tsp (10 mL) maple syrup into each cavity. Place 1 tbsp (15 mL) butter on each apple. Pour apple juice around apples.

4. Cover and cook on **Low** for 6 to 8 hours or on **High** for 3 to 4 hours, or until apples are tender.

5. Place apples in individual serving bowls and spoon remaining sauce around apples.

Double Chocolate Caramel Bread Pudding

Makes 8 to 10 servings

When you are in the mood to splurge, this dessert fits the bill. To guild the lily, serve it with the easy vanilla sauce.

For added extravagance, try using chocolate bread. It can be found at specialty bakeries or by special request at the supermarket bakery.

Make Ahead
This dish can be completely assembled and refrigerated up to 24 hours before serving. The next day, place stoneware in slow cooker and continue to cook as directed.

• *Slow Cooker Size: 3 1/2 to 6 qt*

6	thick slices white or egg bread, crusts removed, cut in 1-inch (2.5 cm) cubes (about 6 cups/1.5 L)	6
1 cup	white chocolate chips	250 mL
2 1/2 cups	hot milk	625 mL
1 cup	packed brown sugar	250 mL
3	eggs, lightly beaten	3
2 tbsp	butter, melted	25 mL
1 tsp	vanilla	5 mL
3	2-oz (52 g) chocolate caramel bars or rolls, broken in sections	3

VANILLA SAUCE (OPTIONAL)

1 cup	premium vanilla ice cream, melted	250 mL
2 tbsp	Amaretto liqueur	25 mL

1. Place bread cubes in lightly greased slow cooker stoneware.

2. Place white chocolate chips in a bowl. Pour hot milk over chocolate and allow to rest for 5 minutes. Whisk until smooth.

3. In a large bowl, whisk together brown sugar, eggs, melted butter and vanilla. Beat in milk/chocolate mixture. Pour chocolate mixture over bread cubes.

4. Press pieces of chocolate caramel bar evenly into bread. Let stand for 20 minutes.

5. Cover and cook on **High** for 3 to 4 hours, or until a tester inserted in center comes out clean.

6. Prepare vanilla sauce if using. Stir together vanilla ice cream and liqueur until smooth.

7. To serve, spoon warm bread pudding into individual serving dishes and spoon sauce over pudding.

Maple-sauced Pears

Makes 6 servings

This luscious dessert is utterly simple but a real crowd pleaser. Serve it at room temperature garnished with whipped cream or a little toasted coconut (page 61).

The best pears to choose for this dessert are Bartletts, with the shapely Bosc a good alternative. Buy the pears a few days before using and allow them to ripen at room temperature until juicy but firm. Rub the pears with lemon juice to prevent them from discoloring after they have been peeled.

This recipe works best in a 3½-qt slow cooker, because the pears remain partially submerged in the sauce.

• Slow Cooker Size: 3½ to 6 qt

6	firm but ripe pears	6
⅓ cup	maple syrup	75 mL
¼ cup	packed brown sugar	50 mL
I tbsp	butter, melted	15 mL
I tsp	grated orange zest	5 mL
I tbsp	cornstarch	15 mL
2 tbsp	water	25 mL

1. Peel pears and core them from the bottom, leaving the stems attached. Place pears upright in slow cooker stoneware.

2. In a bowl, combine maple syrup, brown sugar, melted butter and orange zest. Pour over pears.

3. Cover and cook on **High** for 2 to 3 hours, or until pears are tender. Gently remove pears from slow cooker and place in serving dishes.

4. In a small bowl or jar, combine cornstarch and water. Stir into sauce in slow cooker. Cover and cook on **High** for 10 minutes, or until sauce thickens. Spoon sauce over pears.

Cornstarch

A quick way to mix cornstarch with a liquid is to use a jar. Screw the lid on tightly and shake the jar until the mixture is smooth. (This is faster than trying to stir or whisk until all the cornstarch is dissolved.)

Steamed Pumpkin Date Cornbread

I love to make a batch of this ahead and have it on hand to serve it with coffee. Believe it or not, it also makes a superb accompaniment to Vegetable Chili with Sour Cream Topping (page 148).

Make sure the soufflé dish will fit in your slow cooker before you start to make the recipe.

Make Ahead

This steamed bread can be made up to 24 hours before serving. Cool completely. Return bread to soufflé dish. Cover tightly with foil and secure with a string or elastic band. Store at room temperature. Bread can be resteamed on a rack set in a saucepan filled with about 1 inch (2.5 cm) simmering water. Cover and steam until heated through, about 15 minutes.

• *Slow Cooker Size: 5 to 6 qt*

½ cup	all-purpose flour	125 mL
½ cup	whole wheat flour	125 mL
½ cup	yellow cornmeal	125 mL
1 tsp	baking soda	5 mL
½ tsp	salt	2 mL
¼ cup	chopped dates	50 mL
¼ cup	chopped walnuts or pecans	50 mL
⅔ cup	buttermilk or sour milk (page 183)	150 mL
½ cup	pumpkin puree	125 mL
½ cup	liquid honey	125 mL
1	egg yolk	1

1. In a large bowl, combine all-purpose and whole wheat flours, cornmeal, baking soda and salt. Stir in dates and walnuts.

2. In a separate bowl, whisk together buttermilk, pumpkin, honey and egg yolk.

3. Make a well in the center of dry ingredients. Pour in liquid ingredients and stir just until blended.

4. Spoon batter into a well-greased 6-cup (1.5 L) soufflé dish. Cover dish with foil. Secure foil with an elastic band or string and place in bottom of slow cooker stoneware lined with foil strips or cheesecloth (page 14). Pour in enough boiling water to come 1 inch (2.5 cm) up sides of soufflé dish. (If soufflé dish fits snugly in slow cooker, add water before placing dish in cooker.)

5. Cover and cook on **High** for 3 to 4 hours, or until a tester inserted in center of bread comes out clean.

6. Remove bread from slow cooker and allow to cool slightly. Remove foil. Run knife around sides of bread and remove from soufflé dish. Serve warm.

Plum Cobbler

Makes 6 servings

Sweet, juicy red plums are perfect in this simple old-fashioned cobbler. Serve it with vanilla sauce (page 176) or ice cream.

You can also use peaches or pears in this recipe. Add 1 tbsp (15 mL) lemon juice to help prevent the fruit from turning brown.

• *Slow Cooker Size: 3 1/2 to 5 qt*

7 cups	sliced pitted red plums	1.75 L
1/3 cup	packed brown sugar	75 mL
1 tbsp	cornstarch	15 mL
Pinch	ground cloves	Pinch

TOPPING

1 1/2 cups	all-purpose flour	375 mL
1/3 cup	granulated sugar	75 mL
1 tbsp	baking powder	15 mL
1/4 tsp	salt	1 mL
2 tsp	grated orange zest	10 mL
1/2 cup	cold butter, cut in cubes	125 mL
2/3 cup	milk	150 mL
1 tsp	vanilla	5 mL

1. Place plums in slow cooker stoneware.

2. In a bowl, combine brown sugar, cornstarch and cloves. Spoon over fruit and toss to coat.

3. Cover and cook on **Low** for 6 to 8 hours or on **High** for 3 to 4 hours, or until fruit is bubbling.

4. To prepare topping, in a bowl, combine flour, granulated sugar, baking powder, salt and orange zest. With a pastry blender or 2 knives, cut in butter until mixture resembles coarse crumbs.

5. In a measuring cup or small bowl, combine milk and vanilla. Pour into flour mixture and stir with a fork until a thick batter forms.

6. Drop batter by spoonfuls over fruit mixture. Cover and cook on **High** for 30 to 45 minutes, or until a tester inserted in center of topping comes out clean. Serve warm.

Old-fashioned Gingerbread with Lemon Sauce

Makes 8 servings

Slow cooking this delicious cake results in a moist, heavenly scented treat just like Grandma used to make.

If you are pressed for time, you can eliminate the lemon sauce and serve the cake dusted with sifted confectioner's (icing) sugar. Applesauce also makes a wonderful accompaniment.

• *Slow Cooker Size: 3 1/2 to 6 qt*

1/2 cup	butter, softened	125 mL
1/2 cup	granulated sugar	125 mL
1	egg, lightly beaten	1
1 cup	fancy molasses	250 mL
2 1/2 cups	all-purpose flour	625 mL
1 1/2 tsp	baking soda	7 mL
2 tsp	ground ginger	10 mL
1 tsp	ground cinnamon	5 mL
1/2 tsp	ground cloves	2 mL
1/2 tsp	salt	2 mL
1 cup	hot strong coffee	250 mL

LEMON SAUCE

1/2 cup	confectioner's (icing) sugar	125 mL
2 tsp	cornstarch	10 mL
Pinch	salt	Pinch
	Juice of 2 lemons	
1/2 cup	water	125 mL
1 tbsp	butter	15 mL

1. In a large bowl, with an electric mixer, cream butter and granulated sugar. Add egg and beat for about 1 minute, or until light and fluffy. Beat in molasses.

2. In a separate bowl, sift together flour, baking soda, ginger, cinnamon, cloves and salt.

3. Stir flour mixture into butter mixture alternately with coffee, adding three additions of flour and two of coffee, and mixing well after each addition.

4. Lightly grease slow cooker stoneware and line bottom with parchment paper or waxed paper cut to fit. Preheat slow cooker on **High** for 10 minutes to warm stoneware.

5. Pour batter into slow cooker. To prevent moisture from dripping onto cake batter, place two clean tea towels (folded in half to make four layers) across top of stoneware before covering with lid. Towels will absorb any moisture that accumulates during cooking.

6. Cover and cook on **Low** for 3 to 4 hours or on **High** for $1\frac{3}{4}$ to 2 hours, or until a tester inserted in center of cake comes out clean. Turn out onto baking rack and remove parchment paper. Let cool slightly.

7. To prepare lemon sauce, in a small saucepan, combine confectioner's sugar, cornstarch and salt.

8. Add lemon juice a little at a time, stirring to form a smooth paste. Add water. Cook, stirring, over medium-high heat for about 1 minute, or until mixture thickens and bubbles. Remove from heat and stir in butter until melted.

9. Cut cake into wedges and top with sauce.

Pineapple Upside-down Cake

Makes 6 to 8 servings

This old-time favorite uses fresh pineapple (widely available in grocery stores) spiked with ginger, pecans and orange zest. Serve with a dollop of whipped cream.

• *Slow Cooker Size: 5 to 6 qt*

FRUIT

2 tbsp	butter, melted	25 mL
2/3 cup	packed brown sugar	150 mL
1/2	medium pineapple, peeled and cut in about 10 slices, or 1 19-oz (540 mL) can sliced pineapple, drained	1/2
1/2 cup	chopped pecans	125 mL

CAKE

1 cup	all-purpose flour	250 mL
1 tsp	baking powder	5 mL
1 tsp	baking soda	5 mL
1/4 tsp	salt	1 mL
1/4 cup	butter, softened	50 mL
1 cup	granulated sugar	250 mL
1	egg, lightly beaten	1
1 tbsp	lemon juice	15 mL
1 tsp	vanilla	5 mL
1/2 cup	buttermilk or sour milk	125 mL
1 tbsp	grated orange zest	15 mL

1. To prepare fruit, in a small bowl, combine melted butter and brown sugar. Spread evenly over bottom of slow cooker stoneware. Arrange pineapple slices over sugar mixture. Sprinkle with pecans.

2. To prepare cake, in a bowl, sift together flour, baking powder, baking soda and salt.

3. In a large bowl, cream together butter and granulated sugar until light and fluffy. Beat in egg.

4. In a small bowl or measuring cup, combine lemon juice, vanilla and buttermilk. Add flour and milk mixtures alternately to butter mixture, making three additions of flour and two of milk, and beating well after each addition. Blend in orange zest. Spread batter over pineapple slices.

5. To prevent moisture from dripping onto cake batter, place two clean tea towels (folded in half to make four layers) across top of stoneware before covering with lid. Towels will absorb any moisture that accumulates during cooking.

6. Cover and cook on **High** for 3 to 4 hours, or until a tester inserted in center of cake comes out clean. Allow cake to cool in slow cooker. Invert onto serving plate before slicing.

Sour Milk

Soured fresh milk may be substituted for buttermilk. To sour, combine $1\frac{1}{2}$ tsp (7 mL) lemon juice with enough milk to equal $\frac{1}{2}$ cup (125 mL). Stir and let stand for 5 minutes before using. Makes $\frac{1}{2}$ cup (125 mL).

Pumpkin Pie Custard Dessert

**Makes 4 to
6 servings**

What's a holiday dinner without a pumpkin dessert? You will never miss the crust in this easy-to-make custard. Crisp gingersnap cookies sprinkled over the top add a tasty crunch. Serve with whipped cream.

Make sure the soufflé dish will fit in your slow cooker before you start to make the recipe.

Pumpkin Crème Brûlée

Omit the gingersnap crumbs and refrigerate custard until well chilled (up to two days). Sprinkle top with $\frac{1}{2}$ cup (125 mL) packed brown sugar and broil 6 inches (15 cm) from heat for 2 to 6 minutes, or until sugar bubbles and darkens. Chill, uncovered, for at least 30 minutes or up to 3 hours before serving.

• *Slow Cooker Size: 5 to 6 qt*

1	19-oz (540 mL) can pumpkin pie filling	1
1	13-oz (385 mL) can evaporated milk	1
2	eggs, lightly beaten	2
1 cup	gingersnap cookie crumbs (page 95)	250 mL

1. In a bowl, whisk together pie filling, milk and eggs. Pour into an ungreased 4-cup (1 L) soufflé dish. Cover entire dish tightly with foil and secure foil with string or elastic band.

2. Place soufflé dish in bottom of slow cooker stoneware lined with foil strips or cheesecloth (page 14). Pour in enough boiling water to come 1 inch (2.5 cm) up sides of soufflé dish. (If soufflé dish fits snugly in slow cooker, add water before placing dish in cooker.)

3. Cover and cook on **High** for $3\frac{1}{2}$ to 4 hours, or until a tester inserted into center of custard comes out clean. Using foil strips or cheesecloth as handles, lift dish from slow cooker and transfer to a wire rack.

4. Serve warm with gingersnap crumbs sprinkled on top.

National Library of Canada Cataloguing in Publication

Pye, Donna-Marie
    The best family slow cooker recipes / Donna-Marie Pye.

Includes index.
ISBN 0-7788-0070-9

1. Electric cookery, Slow. 2. Casserole cookery. I. Title.

TX827.P9325 2003   641.5'884   C2003-901458-4

INDEX